The Strategic Accountant

Financial Times Management Briefings are happy to receive proposals from individuals who have expertise in the field of management education.

If you would like to discuss your ideas further, please contact Andrew Mould, Commissioning Editor.

Tel: 0171 447 2210
Fax: 0171 240 5771
e-mail: andrew.mould@pitmanpub.co.uk

FINANCIAL TIMES

Management Briefings

The Strategic Accountant

MIKE PARTRIDGE

AND

LEW PERREN

London · Hong Kong · Johannesburg · Melbourne · Singapore · Washington DC

PITMAN PUBLISHING
128 Long Acre, London WC2E 9AN
Tel: +44 (0)171 447 2000
Fax: +44 (0)171 240 5771

A Division of Pearson Professional Limited

First published in Great Britain 1998

ISBN 0 273 63263 9

British Library Cataloguing in Publication Data
A CIP catalogue record for this book can be obtained from the British Library.

10 9 8 7 6 5 4 3 2 1

Printed and bound in Great Britain

The Publishers' policy is to use paper manufactured from sustainable forests.

Contents

Preface

The role of the accountant in business is in transition. Accountants need to adapt to changes in their environment or they will lose their role in modern organisations. Three factors point to the need for change.

First, there is the rise of MBAs and the 'threat' they pose:

> Five per cent of chief financial officers of FTSE 100 companies are MBAs and hold no formal accountancy qualification. (*Accountancy*, January 1995)

> 'Three years spent in intensive financial grounding may come to be seen as having less of an advantage over time spent on those well-regarded MBA programmes which are interwoven with experience.' (Henley Centre for Forecasting report to the Institute of Chartered Accountants' Education and Training Directorate, Irvine, 1993)

Second, there is the image of accountants. They may be respected, but they have been viewed as remote and non-entrepreneurial. Professor Northcote Parkinson dubbed them 'the abominable no-men'; certainly it is often assumed that they are not equipped, by education, experience or temperament, to take up a role as a team player in the strategic management of organisations. Robert Townsend typifies this criticism in his book *Further Up the Organisation* (1985):

> 'Accountants can be smarter than anybody else or more ambitious or both, but essentially they are bean counters – their job is to serve operations. They can't run the ship.' (Townsend, 1985)

Even David Allen, a former president of the Chartered Institute of Management Accountants, doubts whether accountants are suited to coping with the challenges of the future:

> 'Many accountants are unable to come to terms with subjective judgements about an uncertain future (as opposed to objectively verifiable facts about a certain past) and choose to pass up the opportunity to be proactive financial managers...' (Allen, 1994)

Third, as businesses become more complex and sophisticated, there is an increasing need for more strategic and holistic financial advice: the larger scene, not just the minutiae. Robert Kaplan (1995), captures this sentiment well, arguing that accountants should:

- become part of their organisation's value-added team;

- participate in the formulation and implementation of strategy;

- translate strategic intent and capabilities into operational and managerial measures; and

- move away from being scorekeepers of the past to become the designers of the organisation's critical management information systems.

Still more recently, Robin Cooper (1996), developing Kaplan's theme, argued that fewer accountants will be needed in the years ahead and that those who survive will be those who can adapt to a proactive role in the management of organisations. A similar view is expressed in a recent report from the Institute of Chartered Accountants in England and Wales or ICAEW 2005 working party:

> 'In business, the most successful accountants will be those who are willing to learn new business and specialist skills – some of which will be outside the scope of traditional finance and accountancy. Accountants will only reach senior corporate positions by making a major contribution to the strategy and success of their organisations.'

Accountants need to recognise these pressures and adapt to the more strategic role which is being thrust upon them. Those who do not make this transition will become the dinosaurs of commercial life until, like the dinosaurs, they move from being an endangered species to an extinct one! We believe that every accountant has the potential to rise to the challenge and become a **strategic accountant (SA)**. Indeed this is the rationale for this report.

A word of warning to some of our accountant colleagues. We shall from time to time cast doubt on some of the sacred cows of accounting practice by suggesting that there may be other and better measurement systems for medium- and long-term decision-making. You do not have to agree with us, but please be prepared to keep an open mind. We have integrated a number of emergent accounting practices into the strategic planning process and have signposted further sources of information for interested readers.

Mike Partridge and Lew Perren

Acknowledgements

We wish to acknowledge our debt to the many authors, managers and colleagues who have influenced our thinking over many years of commercial and academic life. We cannot hope to identify them all, but we hope that our bibliography accurately and comprehensively records the published sources from whom we have learned and, in several cases, quoted.

We would also like to pay tribute to the many practitioners and academics who have stimulated our thinking through the presentation and discussion of papers at the biannual meetings of the Management Accounting Research Group.

Our discussions with Wayne Felton, FCA, undoubtedly a 'strategic accountant', were stimulating. We are grateful to Dr Paul Frost for reviewing our manuscript and for his constructive comments and suggestions. Also to Dr Glyn Jones, of Technical Communications (Publishing) Ltd, for his faith in our ideas. Any mistakes or shortcomings are of course our responsibility.

About the authors

The authors both lecture to undergraduate and postgraduate students at the University of Brighton's Business School. They also share extensive experience of devising and delivering management development programmes for practising managers and have done so in Ireland and France as well as the UK.

Mike Partridge leads the management accounting subject group at the university and is involved with the committee structure of his professional body (CIMA). Lew Perren is the deputy head of the Centre for Management Development and is currently researching the development of small businesses. Both authors are active management consultants.

For further information, contact:

Mike Partridge MBA FCMA
Principal Lecturer
Department of Finance and Accountancy
University of Brighton
Watts Building
Lewes Road
Brighton BN2 4GT
UK

Tel: 01273 642591
Fax: 01273 643597

Lew Perren DMS MBA PhD MIPD MCIM
Deputy Head and Principal Lecturer
Centre for Management Development
University of Brighton
Mithras House
Lewes Road
Brighton BN2 4AT
UK

Tel: 01273 642979
Fax: 01273 642980

1 What is the strategic accountant?

From bean counter to strategist.

We can track the evolution of modern financial accounting from the stone tablets of ancient civilisations, through to the acknowledged father of modern double entry book-keeping, the fifteenth-Century Venetian monk, Fra Pacioli, to the joint stock companies of the 1860s and the then new legal requirements for companies to report to their owners. Little has changed in the next 130 years: we are still driving our corporate cars looking into the rear-view mirrors!

Management accounting, not driven by statutory needs, is of more recent origin. The nineteenth century saw the development of larger and sometimes diversified manufacturing firms. With them came a need to disaggregate total financial performance, to identify the cost of output in order to measure process efficiency, to price products and to manage the operations of separate trading units within the firm. By the 1920s, 'management by numbers' had become the fashionable way to measure and control organisations. It remains so to this day.

Yet accounting remains, in Richard Wilson's (1995) memorable phrase, almost entirely based on 'retrospective introspection'. That is, nearly every current system of financial reporting and financial management suffers from two fundamental defects:

- it is backward looking, reports history and uses historical money values;

- it treats the firm as a ring-fenced entity, focusing on internal performance measures and internally generated standards of acceptable performance.

For some thirty years, we have paid lip service to the need for accounting to adopt a future orientation. Yet change is happening. It is instructive to track some of the major accounting evolutions of the twentieth century against the development of a strategic orientation in accounting (see Figure 1.1). In fact, relatively few accountants, in our experience, have adopted the developments of the last 15–20 years (see, for example, Drury et al., 1993). So there remains a long way to go.

As increasingly the measuring and monitoring task is computerised, so it should become more feasible for accountants, as is already happening in some progressive organisations, to become more involved in the processes of management, particularly at the strategic level. The role of strategic accountant (SA) is available for all those who want it.

So what do we mean by SA? And what don't we mean?

- Firstly, the SA is not, or is rarely, the organisation's strategist. Strategy should be a team game.

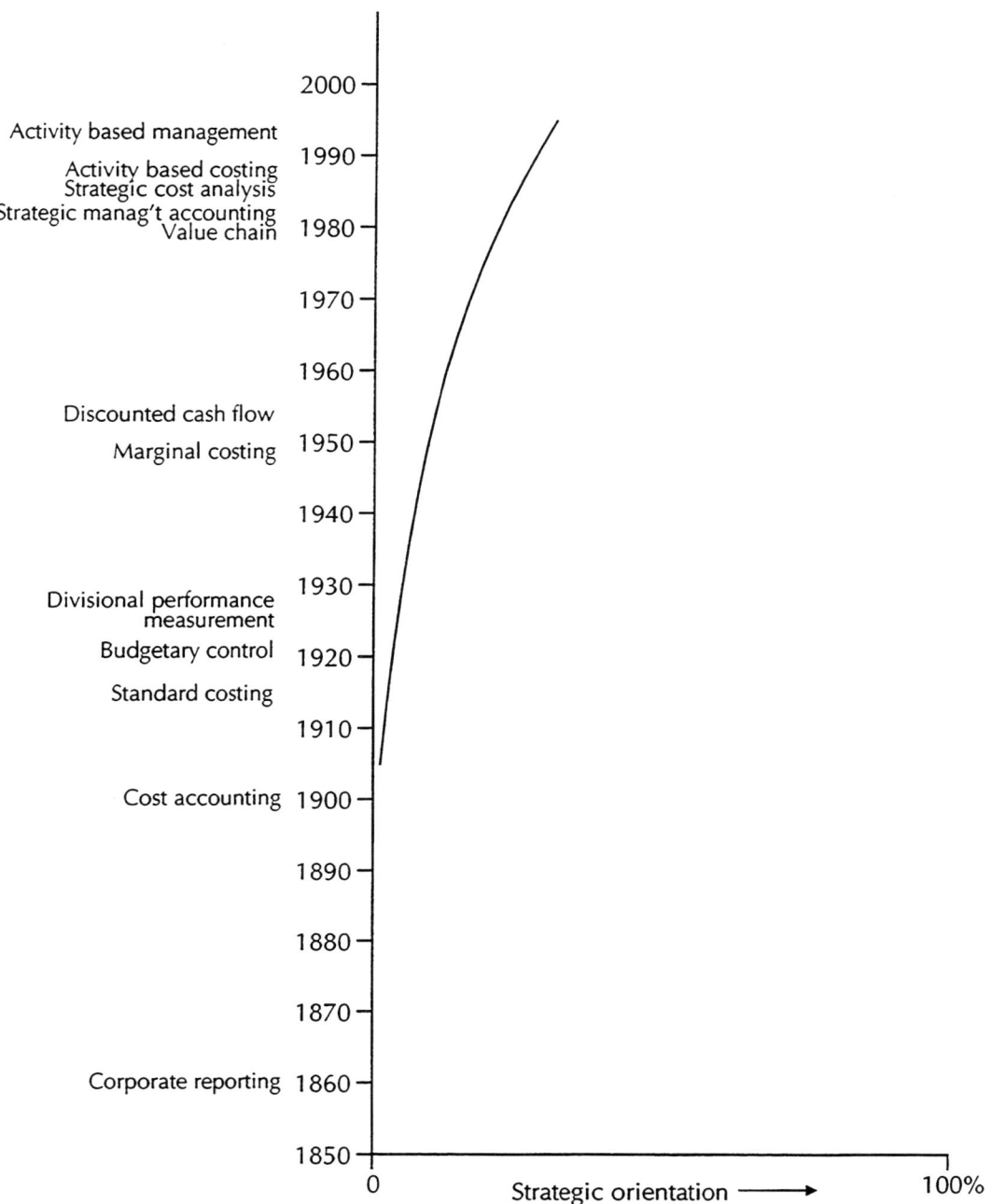

Figure 1.1 The evolution of the strategic accountant.

- Secondly, we do not mean just a practitioner of the techniques that have come to be known as strategic management accounting (Simmonds, 1981) or strategic cost analysis (Shank and Govindarajan, 1993), although these should undoubtedly form a part of the SA's portfolio of skills.

For us, the role of the SA extends beyond the parameters of current accounting techniques, even the more progressive. The SA should become a key player in the strategy team, bringing skills of research, analysis, evaluation and quantification to the process of managing the fit of an organisation with its environment.

We close this chapter with some words from a recent profile of Rosemary Thorne, Financial Director of J. Sainsbury plc (Hopkins, 1996):

'Their role (the chief executives') is to make decisions and take the consequences – hers is in providing the information needed to make those decisions, offering considered counsel and then getting right behind the decision once made. One of the problems in business is that people make decisions without knowing the facts. Which is why it is important that the finance director is supporting the chief executive totally, saying: these are the facts, now let's make the decision.'

For finance director, read strategic accountant.

We have suggested a role for the SA. It is now timely to explore that role in more depth. In the next chapter we shall examine the nature of strategic thinking and how it can be employed to improve the performance of organisations.

2 What is strategic thinking?

'Adventure is the result of poor planning.'

Colonel Blatchford Snell

To understand the role of the strategic accountant we must understand the essence of strategic thinking. By strategic thinking we do not mean the conventional sequential prescriptions that have been so popular on MBA courses in business schools over the last thirty years. Nor do we mean protracted and perplexing planning processes which result in thick reports which are not used by management and which are little more than extended financial forecasts. Strategic thinking for us is simply the ability to adapt the organisation so that it can prosper in its future environment. Certainly a simple definition but very hard to achieve in practice!

'Prosper' is a rather vague word which probably implies some sort of successful financial outcome. This may well be so, but we must be clear that our purpose is to enable the organisation to achieve its objectives. These must include survival, which, for any organisation, requires, at the least, ongoing positive cash flow. Beyond this, there is a wide range of interested parties, usually known as stakeholders, which will include owners/shareholders, customers, suppliers, finance providers, managers, employees, the local community, etc. The parties will have differing views as to the behaviour and performance of the organisation. So we may find profitability, growth, market position, product quality, service and ethical/ecological stance all jostling for attention. Inevitably, the views of the more powerful stakeholders will have the most impact on strategic behaviour. On the other hand, the recent impact of environmental pressure groups on, for example, road building and live meat exports provides a salutary reminder that it can be dangerous to neglect the views of stakeholder groups just because they do not coincide with those of the managing group.

Most of us implicitly think of our organisations in a strategic way. We naturally consider them as existing in an environment of competitors, suppliers and buyers, and influenced by factors such as government policy and economic drivers. We intuitively appreciate the need to scan the environment for opportunities and threats. We instinctively appreciate that the organisation must adapt to the challenges of its environment in order to survive and thrive.

This view is depicted in Figure 2.1, which shows the key factors which influence the organisation: they make up the world in which it lives and in which it has to be sufficiently adaptive to survive and prosper. At the macro-environmental level there are political, economic, social and technological factors. These can exercise a somewhat nebulous influence, but they are nevertheless important. The industry environment depicts the actors with which the organisation interacts, namely suppliers, competitors, buyers and collaborators. These actors make up the arena in which the organisation competes on a daily basis. The organisation is composed of key features such as its product or service offering, its employees and culture, its assets and its know-how. These key features are the resources from which a new future can be built. Finally the different environmental levels can be considered as passing through time from the past on the left-hand side of the page to the future on the

Figure 2.1 Diagram of strategic thinking. (Developed from Porter, 1980.)

right-hand side of the page. As time progresses so the configuration of the organisation's key features must adapt to meet the challenges of the new environments as they unfold.

So far, we have used the word 'organisation' to describe the unit whose future and purpose we are trying to safeguard. By their nature, organisations, whether they are plcs, sole traders, public sector bodies, charities or social, cultural or sporting clubs or societies, are purposeful. That is, they exist because their more powerful stakeholders want them to.

But organisational life is tough; indeed, almost without exception, it is competitive. So we make no apology for focusing, as we proceed with our discussion, on the search for competitive advantage. Furthermore, whether we like it or not, market forces have invaded our public service organisations: the utilities, the health service, defence, education and many town hall services. So we shall from time to time use the term *firm* for the entity which provides or produces products or services which it sells in a competitive marketplace.

Most organisations, or firms, are conglomerates; that is, they are related, or sometimes unrelated, alliances of what are actually separate businesses. Hanson plc, for example, is a well-known example of a diversified conglomerate. Marks and Spencer plc, with its focus on clothing, food retailing and home furnishings, is also, if less obviously, a conglomerate.

So, for most firms operating with diverse products in diverse markets, strategy at the corporate level is little more than portfolio planning: the decision to grow or shrink, acquire or divest,

feed with cash or starve of cash the component parts of the business. It is at the business unit level then that, primarily, we are able to think analytically and creatively about the quest for competitive advantage.

We usually call this unit the *strategic business unit* (SBU): an organisational subdivision with its own market for its goods or services, identifiable competitors and relative autonomy to pursue its own strategic objectives provided that they are congruent with those of the corporate whole. We shall meet the concept of SBU in later chapters; indeed, when discussing the *firm* as a strategic entity, it is the SBU that we shall be thinking about.

The SA will need to understand how the key factors in the organisation's environment can interact in order to be sensitised to the patterns that are possible and to have empathy for the complexity. We will start to develop this ability here by revisiting each of the key factors and building an understanding of their attributes: how they change, how they react with each other and how they influence an organisation's strategy.

Let us start with the macro-environmental factors: political, economic, social and technological, often shortened to the mnemonic PEST. These are not separate factors but interrelate to form complex patterns. To illustrate this complexity, imagine that there is a downturn in the British economy; this may lead to an increase in the number of unemployed, which may cause social unrest and an increase in crime. This in time leads to pressure on the current government to act, which may result in the government spearheading investment in technology. Of course the domino effect of these influences is hypothetical but as far as we can tell, such patterns of influence exist. In the real situation they are more convoluted but the basic notion of cause and effect remains.

Some commentators criticise views of the macro-environment which liken it to a great machine with wheels, cogs and levers that all interrelate in some logical way. They suggest that it is unpredictable and chaotic, more like some strange organism with properties that we will never understand. Certainly it seems unlikely that we will ever be able to predict future configurations of PEST factors with total confidence; nevertheless, organisations have to decide strategies within this complex soup of uncertainty. The way forward is to alter our expectations from precise prediction to broad pattern recognition. It is a bit like the weather: it is hard to be precise about the weather tomorrow, but if it is summer we can be fairly certain it will not snow. Similarly with the PEST factors – we need to look for broad patterns and not expect too much certainty. Some will criticise this approach and say: what about the massive hailstorm in the summer or the unexpected stock market crash? We agree that unexpected events will occur, but you still have to manage your organisation in this uncertain future and the approach we suggest is the best on offer at present. We will revisit macro-environmental analysis in greater depth in the next chapter.

Now that we have looked at the macro-environmental factors it is timely to probe a bit further into the industry environment and how the various actors (suppliers, buyers, competitors and collaborators) interrelate with one another and with the organisation. The more powerful the actors are, relative to the organisation, the less opportunity there will be for easy profits and the more skilfully the organisation's key features will need to be configured.

The most challenging industry environment would have powerful suppliers, buyers, competitors and collaborators that were all larger than the organisation, had more advanced

technology, more established brands, better information, easier access to distribution and supply, and low switching costs. There would be little choice in this situation other than to withdraw from the industry and look for a job!

The maturity and growth rate of the industry environment can also be an important factor in regard to the organisation's ability to prosper. In developing industries with fast growth rates, competition may be low as demand outstrips supply and there is plenty of opportunity for easy profits, whereas in mature industries, with slow or negative growth rates, competition will tend to be higher, demand will be restricted and the market liable to be price sensitive. We revisit the organisation's industry environment in Chapter 4 and make suggestions as to how the SA can play a vital role in scanning and assessing this environment for the management team.

It is the SA's role, with the rest of the management team, to orchestrate the organisation's behaviour and its key features to match the challenges of the macro and industry environments. It is vital to be able to assess the current internal configuration of the organisation's key features, as it is from this platform that any strategic stretch will need to occur. Some options are simply impossible when you assess the organisation's current capability. Chapter 5 suggests ways in which the SA can provide vital information on the current capability of the organisation.

Some commentators suggest that there is a *best* fit for the organisation in its environment, a unique combination of key features which will offer the optimal position (Chandler, 1962). Others suggest that managers have considerable choice and that there are numerous organisational configurations that would allow survival (Child, 1972; Bessant, 1983). What is vital is that the configuration selected creates value for customers by providing products that offer attractive *bundles of attributes* (see, for example, Bromwich, 1991).

If performed cost effectively, competitive advantage and profit result.

Visionary managers can bring a touch of creative magic to the configuration of an organisation's products, services, employees, assets and know-how. They can bring the 'gold dust' of strategic innovation, which results in the organisation having a clear advantage over its competitors. Truly visionary managers are rare; they have a flair which is difficult to fathom but which none the less exists. Nothing we can write here will turn you into such a manager; what we can do is stir your strategic thinking and sensitise you to the issues that your organisation faces. In Chapter 6 we will explore the role of the SA in developing strategies with other members of the management team. We will review how modelling, risk assessment and sensitivity analysis can provide vital strategic information. Kenichi Ohmae captures well the way in which creative flare can be coupled with rigorous analysis:

> 'In what I call the mind of the strategist, insight and a consequent drive for achievement, often amounting to a sense of mission, fuel a thought process that is basically creative and intuitive rather than rational. Strategists do not reject analysis. Indeed they can hardly do without it. But they use it only to stimulate the creative process, to test the ideas that emerge, to work out their strategic implications, or to ensure successful execution of high-potential 'wild' ideas that might otherwise never be implemented properly. Great strategies, like great works of art or great scientific discoveries, call for technical mastery in the working out but originate in insights that are beyond the reach of conscious analysis.' (Ohmae, 1982, from an adaptation by De Witt and Meyer, 1994)

The degree of change that will be needed within the organisation will depend on the gap between its present configuration and the new configuration that is needed to meet the challenges of the macro and industry environments. Many commentators suggest that all organisations need to consider radical reconfiguration of their features using a process called re-engineering (see, for example, Obolensky, 1994). A radical rethinking of the way business is done will undoubtedly be appropriate for some organisations but certainly not all. Other commentators recommend long-term incremental improvements to the configuration of an organisation's features. Total quality management and continuous improvement are techniques often suggested to achieve incremental improvements (see, for example, Dale, 1992). Again these may be appropriate; it just depends on the organisation's current situation and the environmental factors which it faces. It is probably more helpful to take a flexible approach which views the changes needed for the organisation as being dependent on its current configuration and the challenges of the external environment.

It is impossible to divorce strategic thinking from implementation, although many authorities and consultants certainly try. The management of the implementation process and how change is handled is crucial to the success of the strategy selected. All too often there is a chasm between the intended strategic direction and what actually happens. In Chapter 7, we will review how the SA can play a vital implementation role, which should help to ensure that the organisation's direction is clearly monitored and controlled.

We should now have a broad understanding of strategic thinking. We have plotted the connection between the macro-environment, the industry environment and the organisation. We have explored the interaction of factors at the various levels and the need for managers to configure the internal features of their organisation to meet the challenges. We are certainly not suggesting a sequential paint-by-numbers approach to strategy development. We not only recognise that the process will be iterative and exploratory in nature, we insist that it should be. Figure 2.1 presents an enabling framework, not a constricting cage.

It is now time to delve more deeply into the role of the SA and how he/she can take a vital role in developing his/her organisation's future. We will start by revisiting in more depth the macro-environment and the SA's role in investigating, interpreting and evaluating signals.

3 The role of the strategic accountant in macro-environmental analysis

The firm that is insensitive to its external environment or, more importantly, to future changes in that environment is not destined to maximise its potential and indeed may be jeopardising its survival.

The macro-environment, as identified by the PEST factors, and the industry environment (see Chapter 4) offer the SA an opportunity to use his/her expertise in gathering, analysing and measuring information. Indeed, in most firms, he/she will be the person uniquely qualified to take on the role of corporate researcher and so help to ensure that strategic analysis and decision are based on fact as well as intuition.

In Chapter 2 we introduced a broad-brush approach to assessing PEST factors which involved plotting simple trends and taking on board likely events or disturbances. For example, if we take the economic factors, we might look at the general trends through the United Kingdom's Gross Domestic Product (GDP). Figure 3.1 gives the United Kingdom's GDP over an extended period at 1980 market prices. The most striking feature is the cyclical nature of GDP, with upturns, followed by peaks and downturns. It is impossible to predict exactly when the current downturn will end, but the trends suggest an imminent upturn.

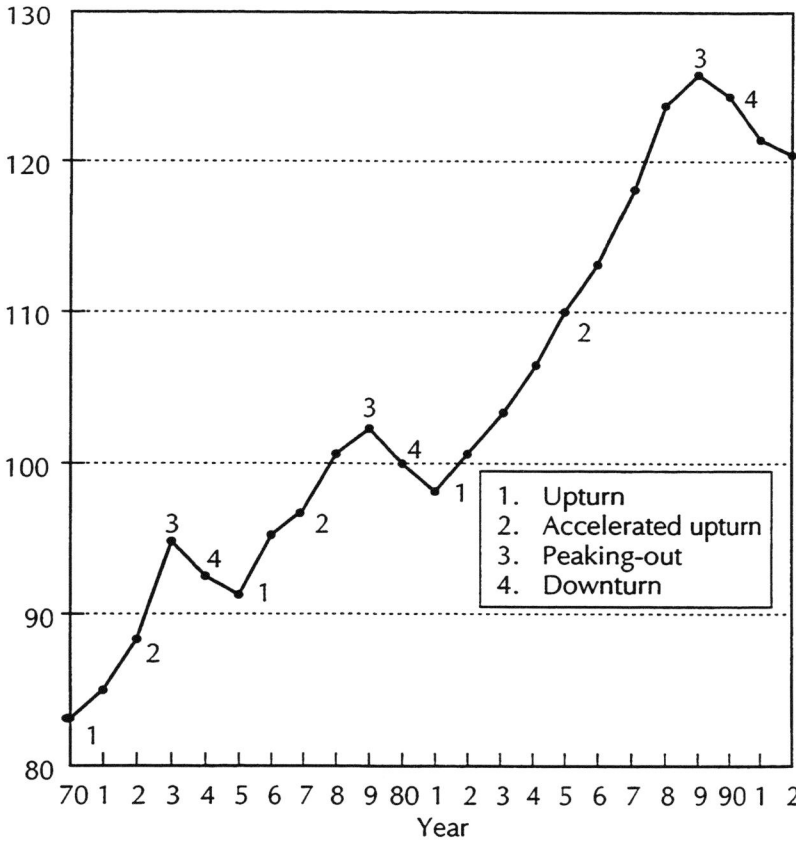

Figure 3.1 The United Kingdom's GDP at 1980 market prices (1980 = 100). (Source: CSO.)

This type of scanning sensitises organisations to the issues and the patterns which may emerge. Certainly they are not precise, but they do give an indication. Similar broad trends can be seen in the other PEST factors. For example, if we look at the interaction of the political and economic factors, we can see patterns in government intervention and economic activity. The level and type of government intervention has varied. For example, until the late 1970s governments mainly subscribed to a Keynsian view of the macro-economy. In theory they intervened to try to offset damaging trade cycle behaviour by maintaining a strong aggregate demand in the hope of stimulating a more steady growth in output and the maintenance of full employment (see, for example, Curwin, 1994). The GDP trends in Figure 3.1 clearly demonstrate a gap between theory and practice!

Now, you may be thinking: what has this got to do with being an SA? I don't want to be a political economist! We don't want you to be a political economist either, but we do want you to be aware of the broad trends that may influence your organisation, so that you are able to operate in an anticipatory rather than reactive manner. The SA should be considering what the political complexion is at present, what is liable to happen at the next general election, how this may influence macro-economic policies and what threats or opportunities this presents to the organisation.

Similar trends can be spotted within the social and technological factors. For example, Figures 3.2 and 3.3 clearly show the increase in leisure time within the United Kingdom. Average working hours are continuously falling and the number of holidays taken are increasing. You will also notice that the number of holidays being taken abroad has also increased dramatically.

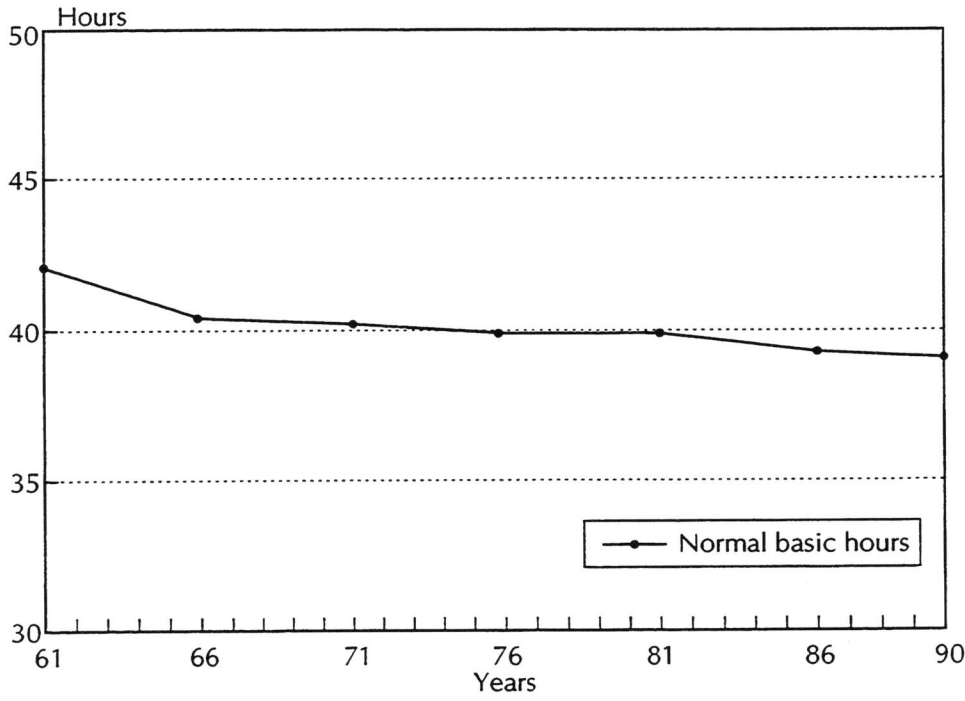

Figure 3.2 Weekly hours of work (full-time manual workers).
(Source: Employment Dept, CSO, *Social Trends 22,* 1992, p.175.)

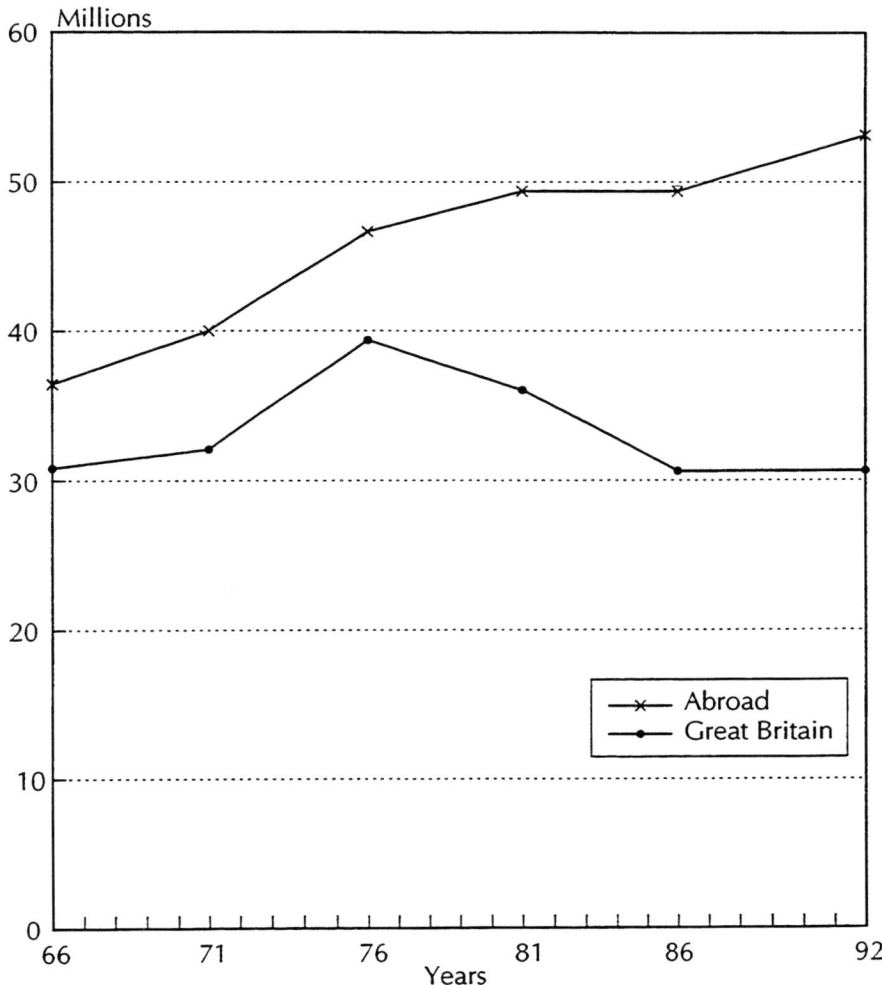

Figure 3.3 Holidays taken by UK residents (of four nights or more by destination). (Source: British Tourist Office.)

All organisations face the same macro-environmental conditions, but the importance of specific PEST factors will vary for individual organisations. However, it is important to think imaginatively about how particular PEST factors might influence your organisation. For instance, the increase in leisure time and holidays abroad will obviously affect the tourist industry, but it may also influence house builders – perhaps there will be a trend towards smaller main residences complemented by ownership of a holiday home. A strategic view of the PEST factors certainly requires rigorous scanning for signals, but it also involves interpretation as to how PEST trends might influence an organisation. This will demand a level of lateral and creative thought.

Although we now discuss the environmental factors that are worthy of consideration, it is important to understand that it is only a subset of these factors that will affect a given firm. And it is almost certain that two or three factors out of this subset will be of immense importance. It is perhaps of some comfort that competitors will be affected by the same set of factors, although their ability to anticipate and respond may well vary greatly.

Many environmental factors offer a threat to survival, prosperity or continuity which must be addressed. Less obviously, they frequently also offer competitive opportunities. The ways in

which concerns and legislation over safety have been capitalised on by Volvo, the Swedish car maker, are the stuff of legend.

It is also worth remembering that a firm may be dependent on the prosperity of, for example, a customer or supplier industry which may itself be affected by environmental factors which do not obviously have relevance for the firm itself. For many firms in intermediate positions in the supply chain, demand for their products is a derived one. It is the demand for new cars, itself vulnerable to a variety of PEST factors, that determines the demand for, for example, upholstery fabrics and latex foams.

Let us now examine the PEST factors in more detail.

Politico-Legal Factors

Governments and trading communities (e.g. the European Union) are increasingly interventionalist. To an extent, they reflect socio-cultural trends, but they also bring their own agenda to the business of public policy and law-making.

The SA should be aware of political stability, or the lack of it, in each country or region in which the firm operates or trades. Hence, the legislative and regulatory plans, and their implication for the firm, of both the present government and its possible successor should be identified.

Indeed the above paragraph emphasises that political, legal and regulatory change is rarely introduced in advanced economies without the alert observer being forewarned. In many cases, there is wide and democratic debate before such changes become law. In some parts of the globe, however, revolution, insurrection and coup, as well as less than democratic legal and regulatory processes, are prevalent.

A checklist of politico-legal factors should include:

- environmental protection;

- employment and equal opportunities;

- competition regulations;

- foreign trade;

- transport policy;

- consumer protection;

- tax policy;

- special incentives.

It will be clear that the relative impact of these factors will vary from industry to industry, as well as from country to country. To illustrate the variety of ways in which political decisions

and activities can affect industry sectors (and can have knock-on effects on related industries), we give a small number of examples in Table 3.1.

Table 3.1 The effect of political decisions on industry sectors.

Factor	Effect	Industry Affected
End of Cold War	Defence spending cuts	Armaments and aerospace
Rise in terrorism	Reduced recreational travel	Hotels, tourism and airlines
Industry deregulation	Lowering of trade restrictions	Building societies and solicitors
Transport policy	Road building	Civil engineering
European Union decisions	New regulations	Fishing, farming and abattoirs
Taxation	Tax breaks on mortgages	Estate agencies, building societies and house builders

Economic Factors

Economic forecasts proliferate, though it has been said that an inability to agree is their sole common characteristic!

It is also true to say that had some recent corporate casualties taken even a passing interest in demand trends and interest rate fluctuations, they would still be here today.

So it should be the SA's duty to scan the major published economic forecasts and identify consensus views, as well as the extremes of the forecast ranges. Factors which will impact on strategic decision-making include:

- Gross National Product trends;

- interest rates;

- inflation rates;

- employment levels;

- disposable and discretionary incomes;

- government spending;

- exchange rates;

- money supply.

It will be apparent that most if not all of these factors are politically driven and so should be viewed as a major product of the 'P' factors. Economic factor changes can affect most industries. In Table 3.2 below we give some illustrations of some of the more significant examples from recent experience.

Table 3.2 The effect of economic factors on industry sectors.

Factor	Effect	Industry affected
Recession	Reduced spending power	Tourism and house building
Interest rates	Dearer/cheaper money	Banks, building societies and house building
Exchange rates	Dearer/cheaper imports or exports	Tourism, motor manufacture

Socio-cultural Factors

Socio-cultural factors fall into two groups: demographic, which are relatively easy to forecast accurately, and behavioural, which are much harder.

The demographic factors include:

- age/gender profile of the population;

- birth rates;

- life expectancies;

- socio-economic groupings.

These are readily available from government and market statistics. And because populations age in a strictly chronological fashion, projections are easily made and remarkably accurate. If you need to know the number of AB males who will reach the age of 65 in the year 2001, then the figure is available.

The behavioural factors are more difficult. What is certain is that lifestyles, career expectations, consumerism and environmentalism are changing. The directions of change are generally discernible; the difficulty is in forecasting the speed of change. Almost certainly, like much environmental change, it is accelerating. It is not difficult to cite some current examples of ways in which socio-cultural factors are affecting industry sectors (see Table 3.3).

Table 3.3 The effect of socio-cultural factors on industry sectors.

Factor	Effect	Industry affected
An ageing population	Increasing need for medical service	Private health industry
Increasing crime	Increasing fear of crime	Security products
Increasing health awareness	Increasingly healthy life-styles	Health foods, dietary supplements, tobacco
'Greenism'	Increase of movements and lobbies	Road building, oil extraction, cosmetics

Technological Factors

We are often told that science has advanced further in the last few years than in the previous history of mankind. Whatever the statistics, technology is moving forward at a mind-boggling speed.

Few, if any, industries are immune from technological change. The evolution of information technology and of global telecommunications technology, for example, can scarcely fail to have impacted on even the smallest business. And it is not necessarily *hi-tech* that matters. Many strategic breakthroughs have been based on recycling tried and tested technologies in novel ways.

The invention of the 'Post-It' sticker was, by all accounts, a technological accident, though it needed the innovative genius of the 3M company to bring it to market. Another recent innovation has been *direct line insurance*, which harnessed the technology of the telephone to an interactive computerised risk-assessment programme – and in so doing threw a complacent industry into near confusion.

The SA should, probably with the aid of technically qualified people from within the firm, seek to identify the relevant research and development spend and its potential outputs at global, governmental, total industry and own-firm levels. There is a science called *technological forecasting* (see, for example, Bright, 1968) and it may be worthwhile, in certain sectors, to tap into the resources of acknowledged experts in the field.

It can be dangerous to view one's technology too narrowly. Sometimes the most threatening technological developments can come from hitherto unrelated areas. Remember, for example, the way in which barriers to entry to the watch industry were lowered at a stroke by the advent of the quartz crystal watch in the late 1960s.

Many, but by no means all, technological impacts on industry are derived from the electronics industry. Table 3.4 lists some examples of how particular innovations have caused major impact on certain industry sectors.

Table 3.4 The effect of technological factors on industry sectors.

Innovation	Influence	Industry affected
Polymerisation	Development of synthetic fibres	Natural fabrics and clothing
Jumbo jet	Development of cheap, safe, transatlantic flight	Shipping and package holidays
Digital computers	Development of text and graphics packages (DTP)	Printing and publishing
Time-keeping through quartz oscillation	Development of quartz watches	Mechanical watch industry
Lasers	Development of fibre optic cables	Cable manufacturers, steel industry and telecoms

Other Factors

There are other factors, which do not fall neatly into the PEST classification, which the SA should be aware of.

Perhaps the most significant are climatic factors which can have devastating impacts on harvests as diverse as wine, coffee and cereals. Global warming, droughts and tempests are hard to predict but, seemingly, are increasingly likely or prevalent. Even short-term seasonal fluctuations in expected weather conditions can have important effects on demand or output conditions in certain industries.

Strangely, therefore, long-range weather forecasts may be within the SA's remit.

The Impact of PEST Factors

We have already stated that all competitors in a sector will experience the effects of the same set of PEST factors. However the SA will be concerned to identify precisely how forecast changes in the external environment will impact on the business. Table 3.5 attempts to demonstrate the relationship between the key PEST factors and the two fundamental financial reporting documents, the profit and loss account and the balance sheet. It can be seen, for example, that sales revenues are, not surprisingly, the most sensitive to a variety of external influences, while interest and exchange rates have the potential to affect reported performance most significantly. Table 3.5, however, is no more than a broad guide. The precise impact on your organisation needs to be plotted thoughtfully.

The SA, having thus identified the most significant or threatening PEST impacts on the organisation, will next wish to go on to quantify those impacts and to explore with colleagues how best strategic action can lessen their effect. Better still, the strategic team should try to develop ways of capitalising on certain PEST effects by turning threats into opportunities (Appendix B suggests a list of sources of information on PEST factors). We shall return to opportunities and threats analysis in Chapter 6.

Now that we have looked at the PEST environment, it is time to move on to examine the players in the industry's competitive arena and see how their behaviour can impact on the organisation.

Table 3.5 PEST impact on the profit and loss account and balance sheet.

	Sales	Cost of materials	Cost of labour	Other cost inputs	Interest	Taxation	Capital	Fixed assets	Inventory	Short-term loans
Employment and equal opportunities			X							
Competition regulations	X	X								
Foreign trade	X									
Transport policy				X						
Environmental protection		X		X				X		
Consumer protection	X									
Fiscal policy						X		X		
Special incentives			X			X				
Gross National Product trends	X									
Interest rates					X		X			X
Inflation rates	X	X	X	X	X		X	X	X	X
Employment levels	X		X							
Disposable incomes	X									
Government spending	X									
Exchange rates	X	X			X				X	X
Money supply	X						X			
Socio-cultural	X									
Product innovation	X	X	X							
Process innovation		X	X							
Energy availability and cost				X						

17

4   The role of the strategic accountant in industry analysis

Most competitive arenas offer what has been called a *zero sum game*. Certainly that is true of those in a mature phase in their lifecycles, when growth has plateaued. In the zero sum game the profits available to the players in the arena are fixed, or comparatively so. Consequently, for one player to achieve growth, another has to suffer contraction. Michael Porter suggests a wide focus when searching for competitive threats:

> 'The essence of strategy formulation is coping with competition. Yet it is easy to view competition too narrowly and too pessimistically. While one sometimes hears executives complaining to the contrary, intense competition in an industry is neither coincidence nor bad luck. Moreover, in the fight for market share, competition is not manifest only in the other players... Customers, suppliers, potential entrants and substitute products are all competitors which may be more or less prominent or active depending on the industry.' (Porter, 1979)

True competitive advantage is only achieved *relative* to the other players in the arena. The power of the players is generally determined by a number of characteristics (Porter, 1980). They will tend to be more powerful when:

Size:	They are large relative to your organisation.
Technology:	Their technology is advanced relative to your own, or you rely on their technology.
Branding:	Their branding is strong compared with your own or you rely heavily on it.
Information:	They possess significant information about your organisation.
Access:	They have better access to markets or suppliers than your organisation.
Switching cost:	They have low switching costs in respect of their transactions with your organisation.

It pays therefore to research this arena conscientiously and, so far as possible, quantitatively. The SA should be a prime mover in this research, working in close collaboration with the marketing function, if one exists. We can depict the competitive arena as a battlefield, with the firm surrounded on all sides with potentially (or actually) antagonistic assailants (see Figure 4.1). (Appendix D gives a list of sources for competitive analysis.)

The relationships are inherently confrontational, whether through the supply chain or between competitors. One of the strategic tasks is to transform antagonists into collaborators (see page 22).

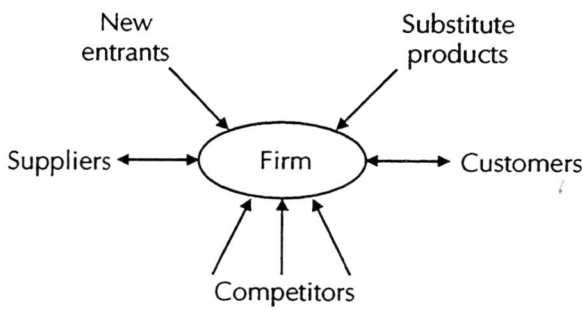

Figure 4.1 The competitive arena. (Adapted from Porter, 1980.)

Competitors

Competitor analysis is neglected by most firms, even though considerable pockets of competitor information are already held within the firm and more are fairly readily available.

A lack of competitor knowledge will tend to accentuate the danger of commercial 'surprises' and relegate the firm to being a follower rather than a leader. Positioning in the market place will be poor or poorly conceived, and competitive strategy will tend to be reactive and short-term in focus.

So what do we need to know? The first question must be: 'Who are our competitors?' While the answer to this is often very clear, it is advisable to look beyond the currently obvious competitors towards potential entrants and those offering substitutes: products and services of a different nature which might offer the buyer similar satisfaction or utility. For example, printed encyclopaedias and other reference works are being substituted by CD-Roms.

The SA should seek to perform a conscientious strategic analysis on each competitor. This should include researching information on:

- corporate objectives;

- corporate culture;

- competitive posture;

- strengths and weaknesses.

The strengths and weaknesses analysis should include an assessment of all resources and competencies, including product characteristics and attributes, and a financial analysis highlighting capital structure and gearing, cash flow generation, liquidity and profitability down to product level. Revenues, product volumes and market share would be a constituent, as would an assessment of accumulated experience.

This is a demanding task but it is far from impossible. A first step should be to tap sources of information that already exist within the firm and set up ongoing procedures that will encourage key staff to observe and source the requisite sorts of information.

Some of these will include the following:

- **Sales representatives or sales staff.** Are they formally debriefed at, say, weekly intervals? They will frequently know the reasons why business has been won or lost, and what the competitors' products or services offer in terms of technical specification, service quality and other *soft* factors, as well as price. This is obviously a sales management responsibility, but it is alarming how often it is neglected.

- **The firm's own purchasing officers.** They are negotiating with the same suppliers of capital goods and raw materials as are the competitors. Their sales representatives will often be more than willing to cite competitors' purchasing patterns and volumes in furtherance of their own negotiations. Again, procedures should be set in place to collect and record this information.

- **The firm's production and engineering staff.** Such people are frequently surprisingly knowledgeable about competitors' plant and equipment, manufacturing processes and technology generally.

- **Competitor catalogues and price lists.** If not already available within the firm, it should not be too difficult to obtain them.

- **Competitor products.** Reverse engineering of manufactured products is commonplace in some sectors, for example the car industry. It is just as possible in most service industries, for example the fast-food or retail industries.

- **Employees.** Employees sometimes move between firms, particularly when their skills are sector-specific, and should be carefully debriefed.

Secondary sources should not be neglected:

- **Competitor's published accounts.** If the competitor is a separate legal entity, then audited accounts will be available from Companies House. Then, depending on the homogeneity of the competitor's product range, broad data on product cost levels and margins may be ascertained.

- **Market research.** This is often available in the public domain: sector and consumer surveys, and retail audits are prepared by firms such as Neilsen and Mintel and are available in public or academic libraries, or by subscription or purchase.

- **Investment analysts.** Such analysts working for the larger firms of stockbrokers frequently publish detailed reports on firms listed on the Stock Exchange.

- **Journalists.** Journalists working for reputable publications such as *The Financial Times* and the *Investors' Chronicle* will publish commentaries on larger companies.

- **Academics and management consultants.** These can be retained to research single companies or industry sectors.

So the problem of competitor information sourcing is far from intractable. Indeed there may sometimes be a surfeit of evidence.

We mentioned earlier the question of competitive posture. This is often influenced by the nature of the industry environment and competitors' stake in it. For example, the market will be fiercely competitive when firms are undiversified and therefore their commitment to the sector is substantial. Similarly, high fixed cost structures will stimulate fierce competition as firms strive to maintain trading volumes. Finally, the lower the levels of product differentiation and the nearer the product approaches commodity status, the more likely it is that price will be used as the primary competitive weapon. This will be exacerbated when buyers perceive little benefit in maintaining supplier loyalty because of low switching costs.

We suggest that the SA should build up a dossier on each significant competitor. Competitive advantage will be achieved by plotting move and counter-move, as in a board game such as chess or Monopoly, until weaker competitors are driven to withdraw or are rendered vulnerable to acquisition. It should never be forgotten that high market share confers market power and hence the potential of high profitability.

The series of techniques known collectively as strategic management accounting (Simmonds, 1981) reinforces this view. Knowledge of competitors' cost structures, volumes, prices and position on the experience curve allows the SA to become a key player in the quest for competitive advantage. Value chain analysis (Porter, 1985) and product attribute analysis (Bromwich, 1991) (see Chapter 5), when linked with good quality data, become formidable strategic weapons.

Suppliers

Key suppliers can be a powerful force in the industry environment. They may be larger than you are and perceive you as a relatively unimportant customer. They will be aware if their products are important to you, perhaps uniquely so, and that switching suppliers would be expensive or impossible. In such a situation, their pricing strategy may be aggressive and their reliability of supply and service less than satisfactory. This is a *worst case scenario* and it may well be that you can insist on just-in-time delivery, zero defects and highly competitive pricing.

Whatever the case, the SA should be the person to work with the purchasing function in order to identify key suppliers and research their strategic stance and power bases.

Buyers

Buyers, whether we call them customers, clients or guests, are the ultimate profit drivers of every business. So it is at least as important to identify and research them as it is the competitors. Most supply chains constitute a series of separate value adding businesses with, usually, only the last in the chain supplying to the ultimate retail customer. So, while it is clearly important to focus on the immediate buyer, one should not lose sight of the fact that a product's ultimate value lies in its ability to provide an attractive *bundle of attributes* to the last or retail customer.

Consequently, we find the well established strategic marketing rule that the product should be designed to meet the customer's need. In bespoke industries, from Savile Row tailoring through to civil engineering, this is indeed the case. In mass markets, it becomes sensible to segment the customers into groups with broadly similar characteristics on bases such as geography, demographics and psychographics. Then products can be differentiated so as to reflect as accurately as possible the tastes and preferences of each segment or group.

It is often said that 'the customer is king'. Indeed the ultimate power of the customer is the ability to withhold their custom. The balance of power in purchase negotiations will swing towards the buyer when one or more conditions apply (Porter, 1980):

- The buyer purchases a high proportion of the seller's output.

- The buyer's purchases from a firm represent a high proportion of their total purchases.

- The firm's products are relatively undifferentiated and the buyer's switching costs are low.

- The buyer has a lot of information about the seller's industry and cost structures.

There is a substantial data collection and analysis role for the SA here. Information about buyers' volume requirements, product variety and specification, as well as their sourcing strategy, should already be available within the firm but will probably require consolidation and analysis. With the increasing adoption of activity based costing (ABC) systems, good quality information on product, channel, segment and customer profitability is becoming available. Be wary of profitability analyses based on gross or net margins or contribution. While such analyses may offer useful evidence, their reliance on arbitrary allocations or on a simplistic view of short-term cost behaviour can make them a dangerously vulnerable tool.

Collaborators

Collaboration with buyers, suppliers and even competitors can create strategic advantage. The nature of the collaborating relationship can vary from loose informal arrangements through to formalised joint ventures where assets are jointly managed. For a collaboration to be a success and to continue it must be a *win–win* situation where both parties gain from the relationship. At first this may seem in contradiction to our previous discussions of zero sum games, but of course it is not; here we are suggesting that the collaborators prosper at the expense of other industry players. If a collaboration is too one-sided then eventually it will break up and battle will recommence.

Collaborations may form for a number of reasons. Buyer and supplier collaborations often involve the sharing of information, design specifications and product details. The aim is to reduce the inefficiencies of linkages between firms. For example, a car manufacturer may share quite secret information regarding new models with its subcontracted suppliers so that they can invest in the necessary tooling in anticipation of the new demand. Competitor collaborations normally occur when both parties bring different strengths and neither would be able to compete as effectively without help. To continue with the automobile example, a

car manufacturer with a good design capability may collaborate with another car manufacturer that has a proven engine to produce a new car. This collaboration may give an edge over the other competitors in price, design and speed to market.

Much has been written about the advantages of collaborative arrangements and cooperation has become quite fashionable in some sectors of industry. Many consultants have espoused the virtues of *partnership sourcing* and single supplier relationships. There certainly seem to be strategic advantages available through collaboration, but there are also risks. It is important to remember that the firms you will be collaborating with still have self-interest and the relationship will only work while both parties think they are gaining. It can certainly be useful to share design information with your suppliers but if they start leaking this information to your competitors or using it against you during price negotiations then the relationship will break down.

Collaboration with competitors can be especially difficult to manage. Quite often the organisation will be collaborating on one project while skirmishing in the market over another. It is difficult for managers from the collaborating organisations to maintain trust in such circumstances. There is also the risk that competitors will obtain access to strategically important information which will potentially weaken the organisation's position in the future. For example, collaboration on a new product may result in the competitors having access to aspects of the organisation's technology which are at the very core of its competitive position.

As markets become more sophisticated and more global, so the need and potential for collaboration at all levels increases. Organisations cannot afford to dismiss the possibility of collaboration, but nor should they enter into collaborative ventures lightly. Such relationships are built on trust, but it is trust built on self-interest, not some form of friendship. We recommend a wary acceptance of collaborations in situations where strategic advantage appears to result for both parties. The SA will often be in a more objective position than the other managers who have worked closely with individuals from the collaborating organisation. There is a risk of personal relationships clouding the judgement of such managers. We recommend that the SA remains objective and monitors the relationship continuously. It will also be important to establish contingency plans in case the relationship should break down.

The Impact of the Industry Environment

Table 4.1 attempts to demonstrate the relationship between the industrial environment and the two fundamental financial reporting documents, the profit and loss account and the balance sheet. It can be seen, for example, that sales revenues are, not surprisingly, most sensitive to the influence of buyers and competitors, whereas costs of materials are most influenced by suppliers. Table 4.1, of course, is no more than a broad guide. The precise impact on your organisation needs to be plotted thoughtfully.

Environmental Factors Can Be Altered

It is tempting to perceive both PEST and industry factors as *given*, pressures that the organisation has to learn to live with.

Table 4.1 Impact of the industry environment on the profit and loss account and balance sheet.

	Sales	Cost of materials	Cost of labour	Other cost inputs	Interest	Taxation	Capital	Fixed assets	Inventory	Short-term loans
Competitors	×									
Buyers	×									
Suppliers		×	×	×				×	×	
Collaborators	×	×							×	

This need not be the case. Larger firms, and smaller ones through their trade associations, can become effective propagandists for their respective sectors. Politicians at central and local government levels are recipients of industry-based lobbying and it is not uncommon for individual MPs to be retained, quite legitimately, to represent the interests of a trade body or industry in Parliament.

Advertising, via television or press, is another way to influence public opinion and social attitudes. Recently, we have seen substantial advertising by the tobacco lobby in an attempt to allay people's fears about the harm caused by passive smoking and hence to reduce the impact of anti-smoking regulation.

All advertising, of course, is an attempt to alter the perceptions or stimulate the needs of buyers by enhancing the value, to them, of the attributes that make up the product. It is sometimes also used to denigrate competitors' product offerings. We have seen, for example, the tables of product attributes, including selling prices, published by certain motor car manufacturers.

Ingenious promotion may succeed in persuading buyers of their need for a product or products which they have hitherto managed to live their lives without. The proliferation of men's and women's toiletry products might be seen as an example of this.

One of the ultimate strategic achievements is to alter the nature of a marketplace, totally and permanently. We call this *changing the rules of the game*. It usually needs a combination of innovative product design, technology, promotion, distribution and pricing (often based on cost advantage) which totally disrupts the complacent status quo of an established marketplace. Whether the innovative firm survives or fails (for it can be a high-risk strategy), the marketplace is never the same again. Timex's $7 watch, John Bloom's mail-order washing machines, Microsoft's operating system and Direct Line's telephone insurance were all massively successful attempts to alter the external environment.

In Chapters 3 and 4 we have suggested that the SA should look analytically at the organisation's macro- and micro-environments. It is now time to take a similarly careful look at the capabilities and resources with which the organisation is equipped to interface with its external world.

5 The role of the strategic accountant in internal analysis

We identified in Chapter 2 that the firm competes daily in the arena that we explored in Chapters 3 and 4. Its ability to survive and prosper depends substantially on its ability to manage its internal configuration, its key features, so as to achieve a *best fit* with the external environment. This will require designed change to its internal configuration.

So a starting point is to take an inventory of the organisation's resources (hard or tangible assets) and capabilities (soft or intangible assets). There is, however, a grave danger of this producing little more that a 'shopping list'. As the SA will be well aware, any stocktake should distinguish between good, saleable stocks, tired or obsolescent stocks and those that are valueless or useless. So it should be with our strategic internal analysis: the SA should classify the key internal factors as either strengths, that is competitive assets, or weaknesses, that is competitive liabilities.

Let us define a little more carefully what we mean by a strength or a weakness (developed from Thompson and Strickland, 1995):

- a strength is something the firm is good at, a skill, an expertise, a resource, a capability or an alliance that puts the firm in a position of advantage relative to competitors and relative to the needs of the market;

- a weakness is something the firm lacks or does poorly, a limitation or shortfall in resources, skills or capabilities that retards or impairs performance relative to competitors.

So strengths and weaknesses should be identified by rigorous comparative evaluation against competitors and against the needs of the marketplace; not, it should be stressed but as is often the case, by a rather casual qualitative statement to the effect that 'Company A is pretty good at ....'. It may be that formal competitive benchmarking should be used to facilitate strengths and weaknesses analysis (see for example, Cook, 1995).

What should emerge from this analysis is a shortlist of no more than five or six key strengths and a similar number of key weaknesses. This process will help to define what is strategically possible in the short term and how resources might be reinforced or reorientated better to address a changing environment in the medium term. The SA is well-qualified to perform this task. Organisationally, the SA is in a position to take a bird's eye view of the whole firm; he/she is qualified to take a view of the firm's financial stability and cash generating capacity; finally, the SA should, by training and inclination, be able to take an objective and evaluative view. The latter, surprisingly, is more difficult that it sounds. There is evidence that analysts can tend both to over- and underrate their, or their firm's, capabilities and shortcomings.

So how and where should the SA begin this task? Because the nature and significance of the firm's key features will vary according to the industry sector and the competitive environment, there can be no golden rule of strengths and weaknesses analysis. What we, and most commentators, suggest is a logical checklist approach based broadly on a functional area analysis of the firm:

- **Organisational structure.** This reflects size, leadership style and the locus of decision-making. It should also reflect the firm's strategic stance.

- **Corporate culture.** This reflects the firm's history, beliefs and values. It affects people's attitudes, behaviour and decision processes.

- **Marketing.** This will include market status and market share, product range and characteristics, customer base, brand strengths, selling and promotional competencies, and position in the lifecycle.

- **Financial.** This will include: firstly, profitability, cash flow generation and profit-volume sensitivity; secondly, capital structure, financing costs, gearing and ability to raise fresh capital; thirdly, financial performance measurement and decision-making systems.

- **Operations.** This will include the type of technology, flexibility and efficiency of plant and labour, quality and cost of output. The impact of the *experience curve* effect on unit costs, particularly in emergent or fast growing industries, should be monitored closely because it can have important strategic value (see discussion of experience curve effects on page 29).

- **Research and development.** This will include technological capabilities and, importantly, the ability to bring new technology to the marketplace; also investment in innovation, research and development and its pay-off.

  Current technologies will in time be replaced by new ones (technological discontinuity) and there is evidence that industry leadership often changes hands at this time.

- **Human resources.** The soft resources are primarily people-based and so here the SA should be looking at the appropriateness of employees' skills, education and experience, productivity and attitude.

- **Management.** Although management can be seen as a subset of the previous item, it may be no bad thing to separate it out for special critical evaluation. Is it equipped in skill, attitude and experience at strategic as well as operational levels? Is it forward-looking, innovative and customer orientated?

- **Information systems.** This should evaluate the timeliness and relevance of information available for decision-makers as well as their understanding of and ability to use the information.

This analysis, when related to the factors that are present or anticipatable in the external environment, should offer the SA a number of messages about strategic action and strategic direction. We shall examine these issues in the next chapter.

The Value Chain

We referred in Chapter 2 to *value creating businesses* and to products as providing customers with attractive *bundles of attributes*.

Michael Porter, an American academic, formalised this concept of the firm in what he called *the value chain*. Porter (1985) proposed the value chain as an analytical and developmental tool with which to break down the value generating activities performed by the firm. It offers an alternative to strengths and weaknesses analysis which may appeal to the SA because of its compatibility with modern approaches to cost analysis and its depiction of the firm as a revenue-generating, cost-incurring entity.

The value chain breaks the value-generating processes down into five primary activities (see Figure 5.1):

- inbound logistics – activities which are concerned with sourcing, receiving and supplying materials and services to the operational phase;

- operations – activities which transform the inputs into products or services;

- outbound logistics – activities which distribute the product or service to the customer;

- marketing and sales – activities which include advertising, promotion, product definition, pricing and channel management;

- service – activities which include the provision of customer service and customer care.

These five primary activities are underpinned by four support activities:

- the procurement process;

- technology development;

- human resource management;

- corporate infrastructure – planning, finance, legal, quality control, etc.

Note that the value chain is not a depiction of the firm along conventional organisational lines or boundaries; indeed many activities will occur across such boundaries and any of the value processes can be broken down into greater detail if such analysis is felt to be helpful.

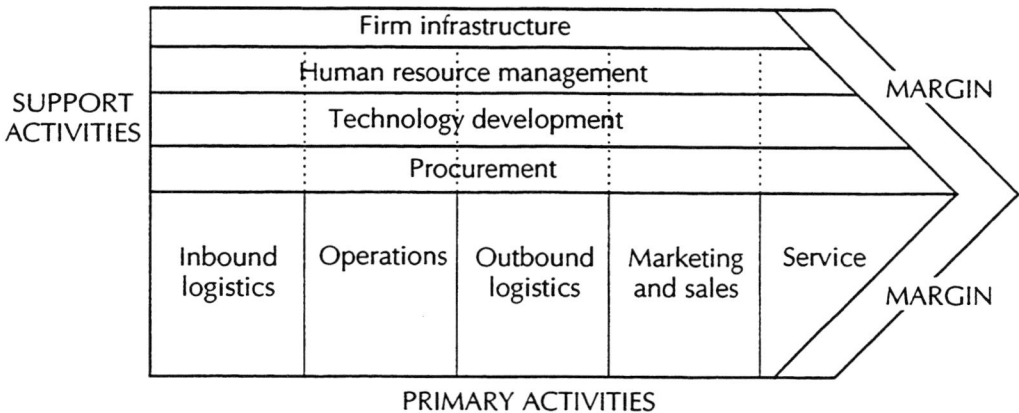

Figure 5.1 The value chain (adapted from Porter, 1985).

Porter recommends that we next look for linkages between activities; effectively, he is saying that there can be synergies between activities, so reducing costs or improving effectiveness, depending on the ways in which we perform them.

The whole of the value-generating chain rarely occurs within the firm. Indeed, we often refer to the *value system* to reflect the fact that some value activities will be sourced from outside the firm (see Figure 5.2).

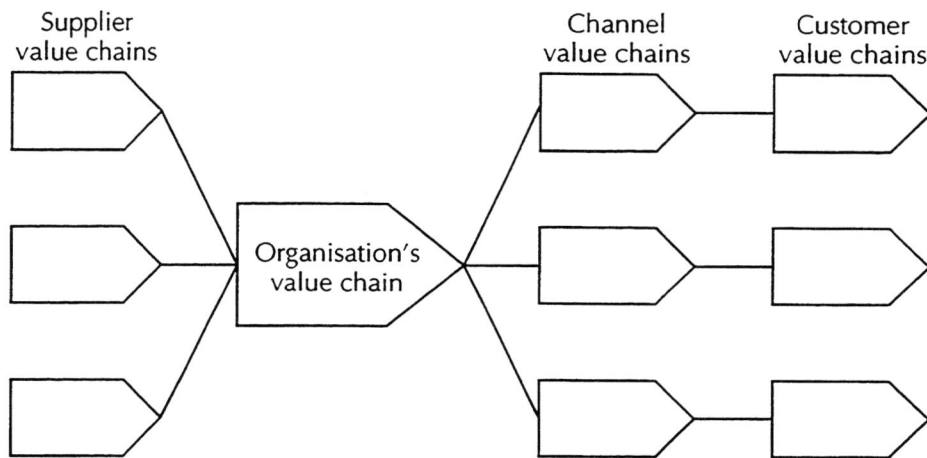

Figure 5.2 The value system (adapted from Porter, 1985).

Paralleling our comparative evaluation of strengths and weakness, Porter recommends that we compare our own firm's value chain with those of competitors in order to identify sources of competitive advantage.

Strategic Cost Analysis

It may be helpful for the SA to view the value chain in profit and loss account terms:

$$\begin{pmatrix} \text{Customer value} \\ \text{represented by income} \\ \text{(quantity x price)} \\ \text{generated} \end{pmatrix} - \begin{pmatrix} \text{Costs of} \\ \text{producing products} \\ \text{with customer} \\ \text{value attributes} \end{pmatrix} = \text{Margin}$$

If we had the ability to perform detailed and reasonably accurate cost and income analysis on this equation, then it would become possible to design an optimally differentiated product, or portfolio of products, which maximises the margin outcome.

We have that capability.

First, we have the ability, given time, to influence the underlying cost structures of each value chain activity. What have been called structural drivers (scale economies, degree of vertical integration, experience curve effects, use of technology and breadth of product line) and executional drivers (commitment to continuous improvement, commitment to quality, utilisation of capacity, plant layout efficiency, product design and supplier and customer

linkages) govern the costs of performing value-creating activities (Shank and Govindarajan, 1993). Any endeavour to alter these drivers can only be achieved in the medium term; consequently we can categorise such endeavours as strategic decisions.

In order to understand and interpret a value chain's cost structure we need first to identify whether the firm's search for competitive advantage, its strategic stance, is based on the attainment of low price positioning in the marketplace, or whether it is seeking a differentiated position, when it may well spend more on generating products with valuable differentiating attributes.

Firms seeking a low price stance should strive for optimal cost efficiency through all or most of the following:

- scale economies through volume gains;

- learning curve effects;

- product design simplification or standardisation;

- material standardisation or substitution;

- process improvement;

- rigorous cost management.

Collectively these approaches generate what has been called the experience curve. That is, unit costs decrease exponentially as cumulative experience increases. It is important, though, to realise that the experience curve does not just happen, it has to be worked for.

The SA may need then to understand the cost structure and cost behaviour of each value chain activity. We counsel against using traditional absorption or marginal costing approaches for this analysis. The former, with its arbitrary and irrational attribution of overhead to cost objects, and the latter, with its neglect of all but short-term variables, are both prone to generate misleading information if used for strategic decision-making.

Activity based costing (ABC) attempts, rationally and causally, to attribute overhead to cost objects and generates, in the better systems, reasonably valid medium-term cost approximations for activities, products, segments and customers (see, for example, Glad and Becker, 1996). We recommend its adoption, apart from those instances where there are major practical or cost objections.

So, using the information generated by ABC analysis, the SA has a means with which to break down the total profit and loss account equation and evaluate the ABC cost of providing (or subtracting) each differentiating attribute – in the firm knowledge that each such cost is a reasonably reliable measure of the medium-term incremental (or decremental) cost of providing that attribute. Indeed, we can go further and use the procedure to forecast the costs of possible future or alternative packages of attributes.

So we can now return to Porter's advice to compare the firm's value chain with those of competitors. In Chapter 4, we explained the process of competitor analysis. The SA should

compare the firm's value chain with competitors' value chains not just descriptively, although that is the starting point, but financially as well. Remember that competitors may be more or less vertically integrated, more or less committed to outsourcing partnerships and certainly differently configured internally. Their structural and executional drivers will differ. Such analysis will identify and quantify sources of competitive advantage and disadvantage and will stimulate strategic responses. It is worth remarking that this process is a form of competitive benchmarking, using activity analysis and activity-based costs as the metrics.

We have so far neglected to discuss the revenue side of the equation. In the aggregate, it is clear: it is the total revenue generated by the customer demand for the product or service. When considering disaggregating the package of attributes, then the revenue potential of one attribute more or less, or enhanced or reduced, has to be a matter of market estimates, market research or test marketing.

In conclusion, let us be clear that strategic cost analysis does not deal in scientific precision. It also presupposes a great deal of hard and detailed work in data collection and cost analysis. The payoff comes in clear, quantified guidance as to strategic position and strategic direction. The SA is uniquely equipped to be at the heart of this strategic information system.

Competencies and Capabilities

So far, most of our discussion of business strategy has been based on the competitive capability and positioning of the strategic business unit (SBU). This widely used approach assumes that SBUs enjoy a degree of autonomy and the independence to pursue product/market strategies as stand-alone operations within the corporation. This has several advantages and it certainly allows strategic thinking to happen at the organisational level that is best informed about relevant external forces and competitive pressures.

Recently, however, it has been argued that this strategic fragmentation militates against the development of overarching or core competencies (Hamel and Prahalad, 1990). The examples of Honda , Canon and Sony are often cited as operating portfolios of businesses apparently unrelated in terms of customers, distribution channels and merchandising strategy. But each owns core competencies: Honda in engine technology and manufacture, Canon in optics, imaging and microprocessor control, Sony in miniaturisation. These competencies, which are in essence unique customer-focused capabilities, allow their owners to exploit a wide variety of markets in ways that offer superior value to customers, outperform the competition and are difficult or impossible for competitors to copy.

Core competencies are unlikely to be developed by chance, but need to be identified and nurtured from a top management level. The dominance of the SBU is counter-productive.

We do not suggest that all firms possess core competencies; it is the star performers who do. However, it is within the SA's domain to stimulate discussion of the issue within the context of internal analysis. It is possible that some set of strengths across the firm's portfolio of SBUs may offer the potential for development of a unique competitive advantage, a core competency.

We have now looked hard and analytically at the organisation in its environment. In Chapter 6, we shall employ the evidence so far gathered to stimulate our thinking about the organisation's future.

6 The role of the strategic accountant in strategy development

Strategic development is at the heart of strategic thinking and needs imagination and innovation. It should be proactive and anticipatory. It involves the creation of a unique configuration of the firm's key features which will match the challenges of its environment and provide strategic advantage. There are two distinct phases:

- The option generation phase, where creativity must be allowed to flourish and diverse ideas emerge.

- The option selection phase, where the options are narrowed down through a systematic filtering process.

The process is often iterative with multiple cycles occurring through the two phases. However, we would recommend that the management team is careful not to trample on the creative thought processes of the first phase with the more analytical and convergent thought processes of the second phase. We have all seen good ideas stifled by criticism before they have had the chance to be explored fully. Carr and Tomkins (1996) capture well the tension between intuition and analysis:

> 'The prime role of finance directors is to contribute to that systematic, comprehensive analysis, but the real challenge in more strategic decisions is sometimes to bridge the gulf between the two separate worlds of intuition and analysis: one so easily precludes the other with results that prove dismal, if not occasionally disastrous.' (Carr and Tomkins, 1996)

The SA's role needs to adapt to these very different phases. In the first phase, the SA needs to form part of the creative team, entering into the spirit of divergent thought and being willing to experiment with ideas. From time to time the management team may require information on the external environment which the SA will be well qualified to provide. This information should be used to generate new ideas and as a foundation for exploration at this stage. In the second phase the SA should play a prominent role as this involves the systematic examination of the options which have been generated. The options should be compared against the information gathered regarding the external environment and the firm. Projected figures should be produced and some form of risk assessment performed. The SA should work with the management team to interpret the analysis and make decisions about the future of the organisation. We examine the two phases in more detail below.

Option Generation

It is important to think innovatively and not to be constrained by history, convention or timidity when options are generated. However, it can be useful to use some broad frameworks which will act as a foundation and stimulus for creative thinking. Perhaps the most popular of these is the Strengths, Weaknesses, Opportunities and Threats (SWOT) matrix. This provides a simple mechanism for summarising and interfacing the external and

internal analyses previously undertaken. There is always a risk of strategy development becoming detached from the analysis and of strategies being generated and adopted arbitrarily and intuitively. We call this *strategic cherry-picking*. SWOT analysis can provide a connecting mechanism which ensures that strategic options do actually relate the firm to its future environment.

Figure 6.1 shows the SWOT matrix. The left-hand axis lists the organisation's key strengths and weaknesses derived from the internal analysis (Chapter 5), the horizontal axis the key opportunities and threats revealed from the external environmental analysis (Chapters 3 and 4). The aim is to boost the organisation's strengths, to reduce its weaknesses, to capitalise on its opportunities and to neutralise its threats. The overlap between each of the groups thus produces four different types of strategic stimulus:

- strengths/opportunities   – maximise and maximise strategies;

- strengths/threats   – maximise and minimise strategies;

- weaknesses/opportunities – minimise and maximise strategies;

- weaknesses/threats   – minimise and minimise strategies.

	Opportunities 1. 2. 3. 4. 5.	Threats 1. 2. 3. 4. 5.
Strengths 1. 2. 3. 4. 5.	SO – Maximise–Maximise 1. 2. 3. 4. 5.	ST – Maximise–Minimise 1. 2. 3. 4. 5.
Weaknesses 1. 2. 3. 4. 5.	WO – Minimise–Maximise 1. 2. 3. 4. 5.	WT – Minimise–Minimise 1. 2. 3. 4. 5.

Figure 6.1 SWOT matrix. (Adapted from Weihrich, 1982.)

The matrix provides some general guidance and it requires a great deal of imagination to generate the potential strategies for the inner boxes. The development of maximise–maximise strategies of the strengths and opportunities box is normally much easier to evolve than the minimise–minimise strategies of the weaknesses and threats box.

Let us look at a few examples of strategic option generation in the automobile industry:

- The strength of an innovative research and development department combined with the threat of environmental pressures against the use of fossil fuels leads to a maximise–minimise strategy to develop automobiles that use less fuel or are battery powered.

- The strength of well developed engine technology combined with the threat of new innovative body designs from other manufacturers leads to the maximise–minimise strategy of a collaborative venture with a competitor that has good body design but weaker engine technology.

- The weakness of poor industrial relations, combined with the opportunity of cheap manufacturing costs from emerging economies, leads to the minimise–maximise strategy of moving your manufacturing base to one of these emerging economies.

- The weakness of too complex a portfolio of models combined with the threat of increasing competition from Far Eastern manufacturers, leads to the minimise–minimise strategy of consolidating your range and focusing on a narrow range of segment-specific models.

It can be useful to consider the following broad strategic responses that your firm can take to the various overlaps on the SWOT matrix (Ansoff, 1968):

Withdraw: pull out of market, e.g. an automobile manufacturer pulls out of the small family saloon market because it feels that it cannot compete.

Consolidate: remain in market in the same way, but improve or refine the operation, e.g. an automobile manufacturer remains in small family saloon market and improves the efficiency of its assembly line.

Market penetration: same product and market, but increase market share, e.g. an automobile manufacturer attacks its competitors through advertising and price to increase its market share in the small family saloon market.

Product/service development: new products to the existing market, e.g. an automobile manufacturer sells 'life-style' vehicles such as sports utility automobiles to existing customers who previously bought small family saloons.

Market development: existing products to new market segments, e.g. an automobile manufacturer sells obsolete models to customers in the third world.

Related diversification: moving into new but related products and markets, e.g. an automobile manufacturer moves into motorcycle manufacture.

Unrelated diversification: moving into new and unrelated products and markets, e.g. an automobile manufacturer moves into newspaper production.

33

We do not suggest that the broad directions suggested above are comprehensive or offer a recipe for the generation of strategic options which will produce optimal solutions to a firm's SWOT position. All we suggest is that they may provide some triggers which may help with the creative process.

At the end of the option generation process, the SA should have quite an extensive list of potential directions. Of course it would be impossible to pursue all these directions and it is quite likely that some options actually contradict each other. We shall look shortly at the option selection phase which provides a systematic mechanism for producing a coherent direction for the organisation.

Target Costing

Target costing is a Japanese response, gaining acceptance in the West, to the challenge of rapidly changing competitive environments.

Product lifecycles are becoming shorter, process methods are increasingly automated and designed to offer a flexible approach to product definition. It has also been argued that as much as 80% of a product's cost is determined before manufacture begins. Consequently the ability to generate reductions in product cost once a product is launched is severely curtailed.

In a highly competitive global marketplace, the traditional Western approach to product cost definition is seen as inadequate. Target costing throws the conventional logic of 'design the product/process, then see what it costs' on its head. Instead it asks first 'what is a competitive market price?' then, by a process of subtraction, the target cost is identified:

Target cost = Target selling price – Required profit

This may often be far lower than the cost that would be generated by a conventional cost accumulation approach to the stages of the manufacturing process. But, by rigorous value engineering (functional analysis) and cost reduction, the target cost can be attained.

As Tanaka *et al.* (1995) say:

> 'Target cost management... differs from conventional cost management practice through its derivation, at least in part, from the market... It ensures that the management accounting system is generating information which will help the organisation to maintain and advance its competitiveness.'

Option Selection

Without a systematic process all the good analytical work that has been previously conducted can deteriorate into confusion, with option selection becoming no more than a political power game which does not really address the SWOT issues. The SA can reduce the risk of such deterioration of the strategic process. The SA's training provides an ideal platform for rationalising the numerous options generated by the management team. The SA needs to act as a facilitator who fully involves the management team by providing information in a transparent and informative way.

Strategic options should be screened against a range of criteria which include:

Stakeholder expectations

Each of the strategic options should be compared with the expectations of powerful stakeholders. If an option will upset a key stakeholder group, it will be difficult to implement and should not be pursued. The pattern of key stakeholders will vary according to the organisation, the circumstances and the strategic option which is being screened.

Financial return

What will be the return from the strategic option? This may be measured in terms of financial outcome or some form of cost/benefit analysis which may try to place a value on less tangible outcomes such as brand value or employee motivation. It is tempting to use simplistic profit-based measures such as return on investment (ROI) or earnings (EPS) profiles. It has been widely argued (for example, Rappaport, 1986) that accounting profit measures fail to measure changes in the economic value of the firm. Indeed, we can go back to 1965 to find David Solomons criticising the use of accounting profit as a measure of managerial performance: 'Only in conditions of unusual stability will profit, as measured in accordance with generally accepted accounting principles over a short period (such as a year), satisfactorily reflect managerial success or failure' (Solomons, 1965). So we advocate the use of discounted cash flow analysis to measure the growth in shareholder wealth, using net present value or shareholder value models.

Risk

Risk is not an objective measure and to some extent it links to the perception of the stakeholders identified above. What will appear very risky to one set of owners or in a particular industry sector will not seem risky to another. Nevertheless, the SA will be familiar with a range of standard techniques which can help assess the risk of strategic options. Perhaps the most widely employed is sensitivity analysis which allows key assumptions to be altered to see what affect they have on the viability of the option. For example, in the automobile industry, a spreadsheet of cash flow effects for a particular export strategy option could be calculated for varying exchange rates.

Compatibility

The compatibility of a particular option can be assessed against the general strategic stance of the organisation. As we saw in Chapter 5, a firm may adopt a low price stance or a differentiated stance which allows premium prices to be charged (Porter, 1985). We also saw how the value chain can be designed to help achieve this positioning. For example, a manufacturer of high quality and high priced clothing could damage its brand by introducing a cheap range of cosmetics using the same brand name. This strategy would be incompatible with the general strategic thrust of the firm and should therefore be rejected even if there was a demand for cheap cosmetics. Equally a firm that is promoting a highly ethical image should not pursue strategies in certain industry sectors such as

armaments, or trade with governments which have oppressive regimes. It is a matter of maintaining a coherent direction and not sending messages which may confuse or alienate customers and shareholders.

If SWOT analysis has been used as the primary strategic stimulus, then the strategic options should necessarily be compatible with the internal and external environments as they are or could be. Nonetheless, it may be no bad thing to test this compatibility with one more iteration.

The screening criteria should be agreed within the management team so that all members feel involved with the decision-making process. It is also important to remain flexible and to be willing to alter the criteria during the screening process. This is not to suggest that screening criteria should be changed just to satisfy political expediency, but flexibility is needed as it is only when the criteria start to be used that their effectiveness can be assessed.

We would suggest a rational approach to the application of the screening criteria, perhaps employing a ranking framework, as shown in Figure 6.2.

Options	Match with stakeholder expectations 5 = high 1 = low	Level of financial return anticipated 5 = high 1 = low	Level of risk 5 = low 1 = high	Compatibility with firm's general strategic thrust 5 = high 1 = low	Total
1.					
2.					
3.					
4.					
5.					

Figure 6.2 Strategic option screening matrix.

This chapter has presented a systematic approach to the generation and screening of strategic options. This approach should facilitate the strategic process, but as mentioned earlier, it cannot replace the need for innovation and creative flair which are essential to the option generation phase. It is this flair which results in a firm having an edge over its competitors and a sustainable advantage. In the next chapter we look at the issues of implementation and monitoring of the strategic options that have been selected.

7 The role of the strategic accountant in realising the strategy

The focus of this report is on the strategic planning process and the SA's role in this process. Many have argued, and we agree, that the process is as valuable as the outcome. The heightened awareness of the external environment and the shared ownership of policies and plans can only be good for the managerial development of the planning participants.

Yet this response to planning uncertainties is in some respects a 'cop-out'. If we value the process at the expense of the plan, we are implicitly condoning the fact that the plan is unlikely to be realised. So we are in danger of setting up a climate which diminishes the drive for plan achievement and allows for its failure.

This is unnecessary. We suggest a systematic and proactive three-phase approach to realising the selected strategies:

1.   **the planning phase** where options are separated into manageable steps, timetables are agreed and resources are allocated;

2.   **the implementation phase** where the different steps are executed to programme;

3.   **the control phase** where feedback on the progression of the plan occurs and adjustments are made if required.

The process is often iterative, with multiple cycles occurring through the three phases. The important thing is to ensure that a positive approach is taken to achieving the plan. Leadership and belief in the plan will be crucial to its success.

The SA's role needs to adapt to these very different phases. In the first phase, the SA should offer leadership to the planning team; the SA's systematic approach and understanding of resource issues will be particularly valuable. In the second phase, the SA should form part of the implementation team, offering support and dealing with resource issues. In the third phase, the SA will play a prominent role, helping in the generation and interpretation of information on the plan's progression. We examine the three phases in more detail below.

Planning

Planning will involve the breakdown of the selected strategies into logical steps. Division into discrete steps will make them more manageable and easier to control. The steps need to be built in a logical sequence, so that tasks dovetail well together. Certain steps will need to precede others, while some may be performed in parallel. Time, responsibility, resource, quality and control elements should be assigned to each step so that each can be systematically managed. For example, a small automobile manufacturer that has decided to pull-out of the general market to concentrate on specialist lifestyle niches might have the following broad plan (simplified for illustrative purposes):

Step		Timescale from start
1.	Identify 'lifestyle market segments'	(2 months)
2.	Conduct review of competitor products	(2 months)
3.	Identify segments for market penetration	(4 months)
4.	Assess potential of modifying current chassis and engines for target segments	(5 months)
5.	Design new body shells etc	(7 months)
6.	Test and adapt new vehicles	(10 months)
7.	Receive approval for new designs	(15 months)
8.	Retool part of manufacturing capacity	(18 months)
9.	Produce small batch of new vehicles	(22 months)
10.	Launch and promote new models	(25 months)
11.	Slowly switch more of production to new 'lifestyle' vehicles	(25 months)
12.	Start to promote new fun 'lifestyle' image of organisation	(30 months)
13.	Start to withdraw old general range	(38 months)
14.	Bring out 'special edition' versions of old general models	(38 months)
15.	Sell franchise for manufacture of general range to third world company	(48 months)

A number of observations can be made: Steps 1 and 2, 10 and 11 and 13 and 14 can occur in parallel as they are not dependent on each other, whereas the sequencing of the other steps is critical, e.g. promoting the new 'lifestyle' image of the organisation before the success of the new vehicles was known would be foolhardy. While outcomes from an individual step may cause the plan to be reviewed, perhaps changing sequencing, timescale or resource allocation, the general thrust of the strategic direction should remain.

The steps above can be broken down further into smaller, more operational level steps. This is what should happen in practice and therefore Step 2 (conduct a review of competitors' products) could be broken down further into the following sub-steps:

Sub-steps		Time from step start
2(a)	Obtain brochures and accounts from competitors	(1 week)
2(b)	Review information and identify 'lifestyle' products of competitors	(2 weeks)
2(c)	Review trade literature on 'lifestyle' products of competitors	(2 weeks)
2(d)	Assess 'prototype' vehicles from competitors to spot trends	(2 weeks)
2(e)	Visit styling shops and design houses to get idea of developments	(4 weeks)
2(f)	Purchase key competitors' vehicles to conduct an engineering assessment	(5 weeks)
2(g)	Report on competitors' products	(8 weeks)

A number of planning techniques, with which the SA may already be familiar, lend themselves to the planning and implementation of strategic options. All of them draw on the basic principles outlined above. Gantt charts are popular: they essentially present the step data in a slightly more friendly way and show the overlaps between timings and the sequencing issues clearly. Figure 7.1 shows how Steps 1 to 6 of the automobile example would be illustrated on a Gantt chart.

Step		Time (months)												
		0	1	2	3	4	5	6	7	8	9	10	11	12
1.	Identify 'lifestyle market segments'	██████												
2.	Conduct review of competitor products	██████												
3.	Identify segments for market penetration			██████										
4.	Assess potential of modifying current chassis and engines for target segments				████									
5.	Design new body shells etc.					█████								
6.	Test and adapt new vehicles							██████						

Figure 7.1 Gantt chart of strategic steps.

The Programme Evaluation Review Technique (PERT) is also popular. This takes a similar approach but in addition allows uncertainty about the times of each step to be shown. For example, steps 1 to 6 of the automobile example would be illustrated on a PERT chart as shown in Figure 7.2.

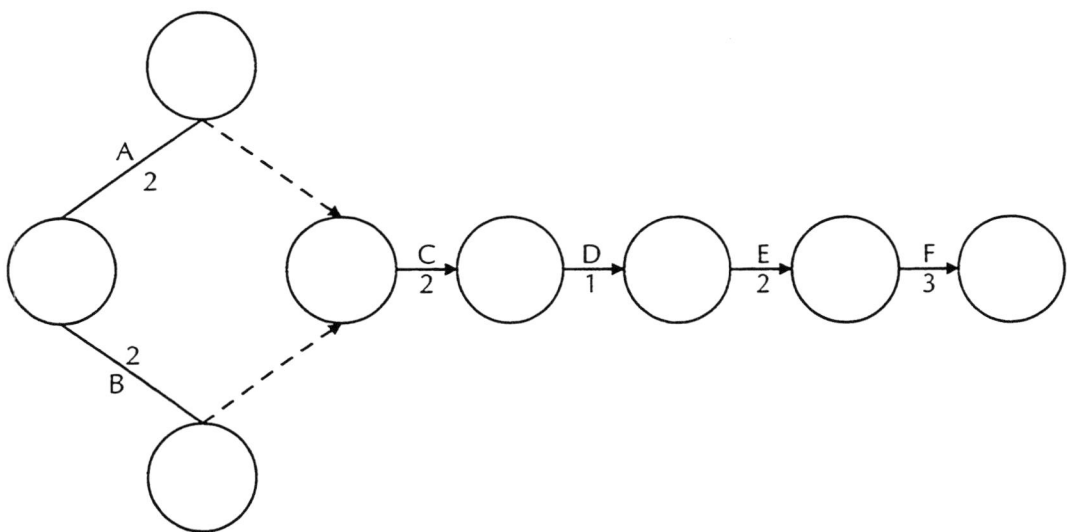

Figure 7.2 PERT chart of strategic steps.

Planning offers a systematic approach but successful execution requires the management of people. This is an art and is where many firms experience problems. Without the involvement of people, plans are no more than dreams.

Implementation

Successful implementation actually started right back at the beginning of the strategic process. It should be relatively easy to execute a plan which is well grounded on a thorough understanding of the firm's position and where options have been rigorously screened for

feasibility. The hearts and minds of the management team will have been won through the rigour of the strategic process. The process should have eliminated impoverished strategies or strategies which represent an impossible stretch for the firm.

Some strategies will meet with resistance from some individuals, especially if they anticipate personal loss, for example of status or influence, as the outcome. Often there are winners and losers from change and it would be naive to suggest that implementing strategic change is always a pleasant business. In Table 7.1 we suggest a flexible approach to change which depends on the current circumstances. Where possible, the more participative approaches are recommended, as they win people over and make them true supporters of the change. More aggressive approaches may only achieve grudging compliance, where individuals comply but are actually waiting for opportunities to thwart new initiatives. This may result in subversive resistance which can be damaging in the long run. Such resistance may manifest itself in hidden ways, such as low motivation, high absenteeism, poor customer service, covert sabotage, etc. However, on occasions when the survival of the firm is threatened, the level of participation may need to be compromised so that rapid change can be achieved.

Table 7.1 Methods of dealing with resistance to change.
(Based on Kotter and Schlesinger, 1979.)

Approach	Commonly used in situations
Education and communication	Where there is a lack of information or inaccurate information and analysis.
Participation and involvement	Where the instigators do not have all the information they need to design the change, and where others have considerable power.
Facilitation and support	Where people are resistant because of adjustment problems.
Negotiation and agreement	Where someone or some group will clearly lose out in a change, and where that group has considerable power to resist.
Manipulation	Where other tactics will not work, or are too expensive.
Explicit and implicit coercion	Where speed is essential and the change initiators possess considerable power.

It can be useful to consider the forces *for* and *against* a strategic change in an analytical way, the aim being to support forces *for* the strategic change and to neutralise those *against* (Lewin, 1974). The automobile example discussed earlier can be illustrated in this way:

Force against change			Forces for change
Some job losses	→	←	Old range uncompetitive
Need for new skills	→	←	Impossible to achieve sufficient economies of scale
Equipment obsolescence	→	←	Diminishing market
Damaged image of old models	→	←	Increasing demand for 'lifestyle' products
High financial investment	→	←	Specialist design and production skills
Dealers needing to change	→	←	Potential for global market
Markets	→	←	Possible 'spin-offs' to other 'lifestyle' products

The management team should try to minimise the forces *against* change. For example, the problems with job losses could be alleviated by retraining staff to work on the new vehicles, and by explaining that, if the strategy is successful, new jobs should be created and generous redundancy will be offered. Forces *for* the change should be maximised. For example, the message of increased demand for these new 'lifestyle' vehicles should be conveyed to employees and dealers so as to help win their commitment to the change.

Control

As with all planning systems, we should seek to complete the feedback and control loops so that all the players in the process are informed and motivated towards plan achievement and so that deviations are monitored and acted upon.

The SA will already be saying 'that sounds suspiciously like budgetary control to me' and, to a degree, that is so. Given that the annual budget should be the first-year run-off of the strategic plan, then the familiar processes of monthly operating statements and variance reports will indeed be a part of our short-term management of the future. But there is more to it than that.

We suggest (developing work from Pearce and Robinson, 1994) that there are three levels of control question that the SA needs to ask.

Assumptions about the External Environment

Are the external environment and the industry environment behaving as we had anticipated? Are the premises and assumptions on which we built our strategy still going to come to pass?

This implies an ongoing level of broad environmental and industry scanning with deviations and trends monitored and reported at frequent intervals. It is also important that this scanning is especially alert for the early warning signs of environmental 'surprises', those often major and largely unforeseen external forces whose impacts can affect whole industries.

Strategic 'Milestones'

The SA should also assume responsibility for monitoring the outcomes of strategic actions and their effects. This can include management of the physical and human dimensions of the implementation of new strategic ventures, and getting the resources and system changes into place to agreed timescales and cost levels.

It should also include the ongoing monitoring of strategic actions and their outcomes over years, rather than just the months of the implementation phase. A good strategic plan will include achievement 'milestones' and it is these that should be measured, in terms of time, value and other strategic outcomes.

The SA will observe that there can be a cause and effect relationship between these first two control issues: variations from environmental expectations can affect the achievement of planned strategic outcomes. But so also can internal performance failures.

So we recommend that, at least to start with, the two control questions are reported separately and the temptation to excuse all outcome variations by citing a changing

environment is avoided. At some stage this issue will need to be addressed and a decision to go on, adjust or even abort the strategy will need to be taken. Because of the critical nature of these reports, in terms of both time and strategic achievement, we recommend that a part of each monthly board meeting is set aside for a review of the issues revealed. Strategic survival is too important to be subordinated to firefighting!

Performance Measurement

The third strategic control issue is that of operational performance measurement, or management. This is an aspect that has tended to be poorly monitored in many firms. There are several reasons for this:

- There is frequently little planned correlation between operational performance and strategic thrust or direction.

- There is often a tendency to focus on 'easy to measure', rather than 'important to measure', metrics.

- The metrics used have tended to bias managers' behaviour towards short-termism, parochialism, even manipulation, at the expense of strategic objectives.

- Probably because they are readily available, financial profit measures have tended to predominate.

A well-known saying in this context is that 'what you measure is what you get'. And there is little doubt that if you measure, or reward, managers on budget achievement, profit performance or return on investment (ROI) ratios, that is what they will manage, or manipulate, their operations to achieve. Similarly, many standard cost variances can motivate sub-optimal behaviour: purchasing inferior materials, performing unwanted operations to improve volume or efficiency variances, and so on.

Our conclusion from this analysis is to recommend a performance measurement system with two essential characteristics: firstly, it should derive in a direct causal line from your strategic objectives (developed from Cooper, 1993):

Strategic objectives
↓
Chosen strategies
↓
Critical (or key) success factors (CSFs)
↓
Key Performance Indicators (KPIs)

In this schema the CSFs should be the three or four factors which are fundamental to the achievement of each particular strategic objective. KPIs translate the appraisal of CSF achievement into quantifiable measures. We shall give an illustration of this process in a moment.

Secondly, CSFs and KPIs should be multi-dimensional so as to reflect the full spectrum of strategic goals and to prevent managers from focusing on a single dimension to the neglect of others. Chapters 2 and 6 introduced the need for our chosen strategies to match with stakeholder expectations. In practice, this will mean that the strategies have to satisfy multiple criteria, e.g. EPS growth for shareholders, survival and security for employees and quality and service for customers.

Robert Kaplan and David Norton have suggested a *balanced scorecard* approach which combines financial measures with operational, organisational innovation and customer service measures (see Figure 7.3).

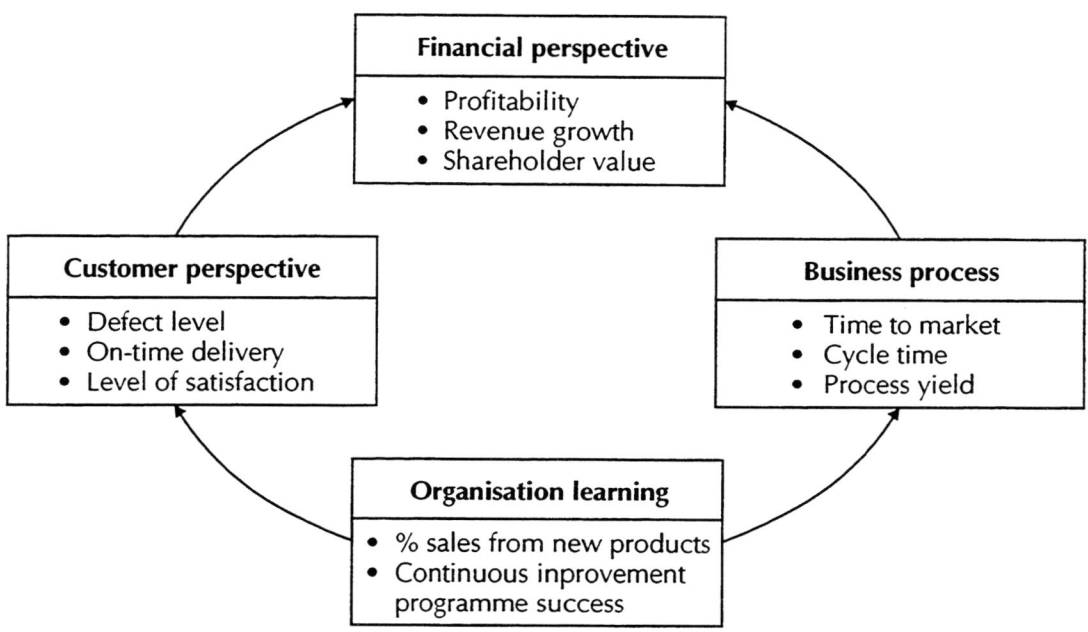

Figure 7.3 The balanced scorecard.
(Adapted from Kaplan and Norton, 1992.)

The balanced scorecard becomes the manager's instrument panel for managing the complexity of the organisation. We have developed in Figure 7.4 an extract from an imaginary balanced scorecard performance management system which demonstrates the role of CSFs and KPIs in the process.

Note that this example is incomplete: there would need to be a wider array of CSFs and KPIs which would also need to be 'cascaded' down through the layers of management.

As noted in Chapter 6, we recommend that consideration be given to use of shareholder value measurement techniques when evaluating strategic options. If shareholder wealth creation is the fundamental objective of firms in capitalist economies, then this is the measure that we should use not only when selecting strategic options but also when evaluating their subsequent performance. An increasing number of US companies, including for example, Coca-Cola, AT&T and Quaker Oats, are enthusiastic users of the approach. For further reading see Rappaport (1986) and Tulley (1993).

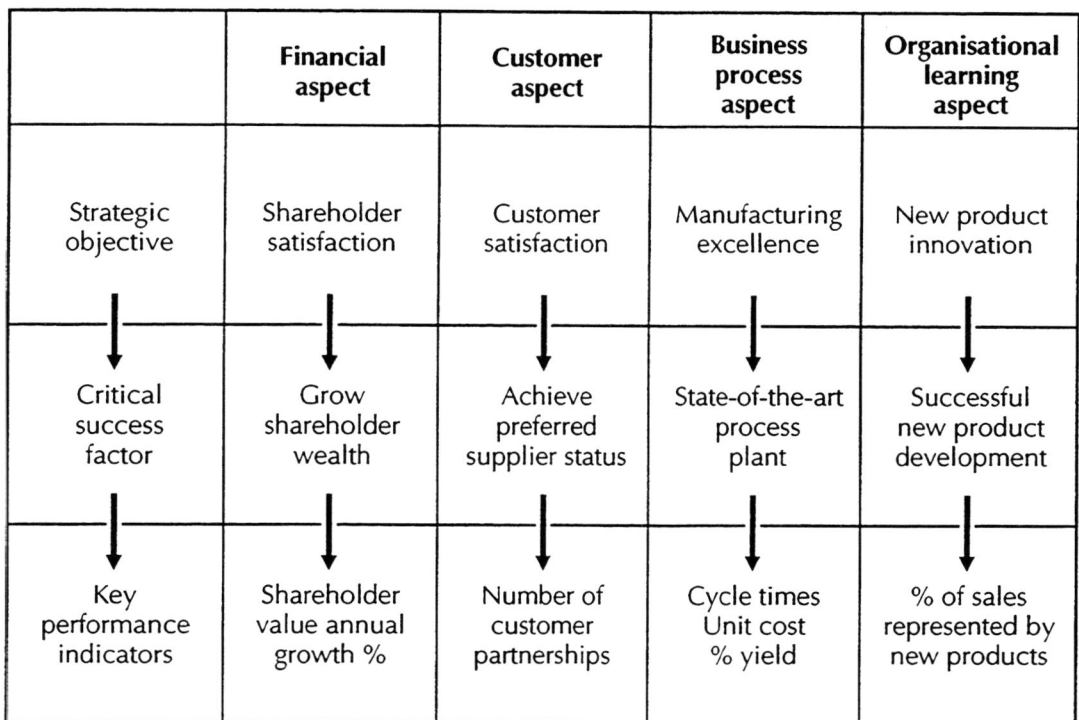

	Financial aspect	Customer aspect	Business process aspect	Organisational learning aspect
Strategic objective	Shareholder satisfaction	Customer satisfaction	Manufacturing excellence	New product innovation
Critical success factor	Grow shareholder wealth	Achieve preferred supplier status	State-of-the-art process plant	Successful new product development
Key performance indicators	Shareholder value annual growth %	Number of customer partnerships	Cycle times Unit cost % yield	% of sales represented by new products

Figure 7.4 A balanced scorecard performance management system. (Developed from Kaplan and Norton 1992, 1996.)

Fitzgerald *et al.* (1993) argue for a six factor scorecard which separates the *results* of action from the *determinants* of those results. Thus, quality of service, flexibility, resource utilization and innovation represent the means whereby competitive success is achieved. Their full scorecard is given in Figure 7.5.

Although developed in a service industry context, the approach has intuitive appeal and could, with minor amendments, be applied for use in many business areas.

The difficulty of implementing a strategically relevant balanced scorecard approach should not be underestimated. It will require managers to alter their focus from traditional functions and departments towards customers and activities. It requires the involvement of all senior managers and, although the SA can usefully act as the design coordinator, its scope goes much wider than the finance function and its reporting mechanisms. At its best, it will mean that all managers, and all parts of the firm, are pulling together towards the achievement of strategic goals, and are being monitored on this endeavour. Internal or competitive benchmarking of selected KPIs will help to complete the picture.

We have now completed the process. The SA should be monitoring the achievement of the strategies that have been implemented and which represent a logical and achievable route towards realising the major stakeholders' objectives for the organisation.

In the final chapter we shall, through the medium of a self-administered checklist, attempt to steer the reader along the path toward becoming a **strategic accountant**.

	Dimensions of performance	Types of measures
R E S U L T S	Competitiveness	Relative market share and position Sales growth Measures of the customer base
	Financial performance	Cash flows Shareholder value Gearing Market ratios
D E T E R M I N A N T S	Quality of service	Reliability Responsiveness Aesthetics/appearance Cleanliness/tidiness Comfort Friendliness Communication Courtesy Competence Access Availability Security
	Flexibility	Volume flexibility Delivery speed flexibility Specification flexibility
	Resource utilisation	Productivity Efficiency
	Innovation	Performance of the innovation process Performance of individual innovations

Figure 7.5 Performance measurements across six dimensions. (Adapted from Fitzgerald *et al.,* 1993.)

8 The future of the strategic accountant

In the opening chapter we explored the way in which the role of the accountant has evolved over the last two centuries to the point where every accountant now has the opportunity to become his/her organisation's SA. In subsequent chapters we explored the role of the SA from macro-environmental analysis through to strategy realisation. In each chapter we identified opportunities for the SA to use his/her expertise to aid the strategy process. Indeed, in most firms, he/she was felt to be uniquely qualified to take on the tasks, and so to help ensure that the strategic process was based on sound information and a methodical approach.

The role of accountants has expanded over the years, but only a minority are truly operating as SAs. In this final chapter we suggest that you audit your own role as an SA. We also suggest tactics to increase your involvement in the strategy process. The questionnaire (Appendix A) asks you to score your present involvement in the strategic tasks that have been presented in the previous chapters. When you have completed the questionnaire, we will evaluate your current position, all the way from non-strategic record-keeper through to SA.

We suggest a ranking, Table 8.1, which, we must stress, offers no more than a broad indication of your involvement of the strategy of your organisation.

Table 8.1 SA questionnaire ranking.

Score	Description
50 plus	You are an SA who is probably leading the strategy process of your firm.
30 – 49	You are an SA who is fully involved in the strategy process of your firm.
15 – 29	You have a high level of involvement in the strategy process of your firm and are probably evolving into an SA.
7 – 14	You have a number of strategic tasks that are important to the firm.
4 – 6	You have some strategic input but it is slight.
0 – 3	You are not very involved in the strategic direction of your firm and probably mainly perform a standard record-keeping function.

We want all readers of this report to become more strategically involved, as we believe that accountants are uniquely placed to help firms with their strategic processes. So wherever you find yourself on the ranking, our objective is to move you up further. We suggest that in most organisations this will best be achieved through an incremental rather than an aggressive approach towards obtaining more involvement. The management team is more likely to accept the accountant undertaking specific strategic tasks, especially those involving financial or quantitative research, than they are the accountant asking to be responsible for the whole strategic process.

We suggest that you review your responses to the questionnaire and identify strategic tasks that you do not currently perform and which you feel the management team would find acceptable for you to perform. It may be that a particular task is not performed at all at present or that the manager that is currently performing the task finds it difficult or

inconvenient. By subsuming these tasks into your role you will slowly raise your profile and involvement in the strategic process. You will also find yourself invited to strategic meetings, if you are not already.

We hope you have found this report thought provoking and that it will motivate you to enhance your involvement in the strategic process within your firm. We believe this will not only benefit your career but also improve your firm's ability to adapt to its future environment.

Appendix A Strategic task self-assessment

Strategic tasks	Score 0 = No involvement 1 = Some involvement 2 = Full involvement
Assessment of effects of government fiscal policies	
Assessment of effects of changes in accounting standards	
Assessment of effect of general political factors	
Assessment of effect of general economic factors	
Assessment of effect of general social factors	
Assessment of effect of general technological factors	
Assessment of competitor strengths and weaknesses	
Assessment of suppliers	
Assessment of customers	
Assessment of collaborators	
Assessment of potential takeovers or mergers	
Coordination of budget preparation and control	
Provision of strategic financial information for senior managers	
Assessment of your firm's financial strengths and weaknesses	
Assessment of your firm's operational strengths and weaknesses	
Assessment of your firm's people strengths and weaknesses	
Assessment of your firm's information systems	
Option generation	
Financial aspects of option screening	
Other aspects of option screening	
Production of tactical plans for strategy implementation	
Coordination and control of strategic plans	
Change management aspects of implementation	
Establishment of critical success factors	
Performance measurement directly related to planned strategic achievement	
Introduction of activity based costing or management systems	
Introduction of business process re-engineering	
Introduction of total quality management	
Introduction of BS 5750/ISO 9000 quality standards	
Introduction of materials requirement planning	
Introduction of just-in-time	
Introduction of new management information systems	
Total	

Appendix B Glossary of terms

Activity based costing (ABC)
A costing technique that uses the benefits received from activities as the basis for allocating costs to cost objects.

Attributes
Aspects of a product's configuration, tangible and intangible, which offer the customer perceived utility and therefore value.

Balanced scorecard
An approach to performance measurement developed by Robert Kaplan and David Norton which suggests mixing financial and non-financial measures across four dimensions:

- financial perspective;
- customer perspective;
- internal business perspective;
- innovation and learning perspective.

Benchmarking
The process of measuring the performance of products or activities against best levels, whether from within or outside the organisation.

Brand identity
Consumer's perceptions and belief in the characteristics inherent in a brand which manifest themselves as brand loyalty.

Competitive analysis
A systematic approach to analysing competitors' strengths, weaknesses and competitive position as an aid to designing strategy.

Continuous improvement
The process which focuses the energies of people in the organisation towards incremental improvement in the internal activities of the organisation.

Economies of scale
The reduction in unit cost as output is increased.

Entry barriers
Those factors which render it difficult for a firm to enter an established industry sector, e.g. high start-up costs or special skills and knowledge.

Exit barriers
Those factors that prevent firms from leaving their current industry sector, e.g. investment in specialist equipment.

Experience curve
An arithmetical relationship which describes how total costs per product unit may decline exponentially as cumulative volume increases.

Learning curve
An arithmetical relationship which describes how unit labour time may decline as cumulative volume increases.

Linkages
Relationships between value chain activities, usually seen as offering the potential for improved economy or effectiveness.

Outsourcing
The purchasing of goods or services from outside suppliers, in preference to supplying them from within the firm.

PERT	Programme evaluation and review technique (PERT) is a method of displaying a project as a network of interrelated activities.
Re-engineering	Radically rethinking the activities in an organisation that combine to produce value for customers.
Shareholder value analysis	An approach to decision-making and performance evaluation based on measuring, using a discounted cash flow approach, the wealth created for shareholders.
Stakeholders	Individuals and groups who have a concern for the prosperity and/or the behaviour of an organisation.
Strategic business unit (SBU)	A firm, or subdivision of a firm, for which separate competitive strategies can be developed and implemented. Usually most of the following apply:

- the unit is autonomous;
- it is profit responsible;
- it has its own market segment and competitors.

Strategic management accounting	'The provision and analysis of management accounting data about a business and its competitors for use in developing and monitoring business strategy' (Simmonds, 1981).
Strategic plan	The explanation by the management team of the direction they intend the organisation will take over a given period of time.
Strategic planning	A formal process by which the management team decide the direction they intend the organisation should take over a given period of time.
Substitute product	A product that is perceived by the customer as satisfying the same need.
Switching costs	The costs of changing from an existing way of operating to a new one, e.g. a car manufacturer switching from one component supplier to another may incur retooling and set-up costs.
SWOT	A summary of the organisation's strengths and weaknesses, and the external opportunities and threats it faces.
Total quality management	The process of empowering all members of the organisation to improve all aspects of business operations.
Value chain	The sequence of direct and support activities which combine to add utility and therefore value to the product.
Value system	The wider system of value adding activities which includes activities performed outside the organisation.
Vertical integration	The combining in one firm of two or more vertically related activities, e.g. oil extraction, oil refinery and retail sales of petrol.

Appendix C References

The following texts and articles were consulted during the writing of this report:

Accountancy (1995) 'Still a quality qualification', *Accountancy*, January.

Allen, D. (1994) *Strategic Financial Decisions*, Kogan Page.

Ansoff, H.I. (1968) *Corporate Strategy*, Penguin.

Bessant, J. (1983) 'Management and manufacturing innovation: the case of information technology', in G. Winch (ed.) *Information Technology in Manufacturing Processes*, Rosendale.

Bright, J.F. (ed.) (1968) *Technological Forecasting for Industry and Government*, Prentice Hall.

Bromwich, M. (1991) 'Accounting information for strategic excellence', in O.G. Okonomistyring, *Strategic–Nyeideer Nye erfarinjer*, Systime Denmark.

Bromwich, M. and Bhimani, A. (1994) *Management Accounting: Pathways to Progress*, CIMA.

Carr, C. and Tomkins, C. (1996) 'Strategic investment decisions: the importance of SCM. A comparative analysis of 51 case studies in UK, US and German companies', *Management Accounting Research*, Vol. 7.

Chandler, A.D. (1962) *Strategy and Structure*, M.I.T. Press, Cambridge, Mass.

Child, J. (1972) 'Organisational structure, environment and performance: the role of strategic choice', *Sociology*, Vol. 6, No. 1.

Cook, S. (1995) *Practical Benchmarking*, Kogan Page.

Cooper, G. (1993) 'Performance Measurement', a paper presented to the Management Accountancy Research Group Conference, London School of Economics, April.

Cooper, R. (1996) 'The changing practice of management accounting', *Management Accounting* (UK), Vol. 74, No. 3.

Curwin, P. (1994) *Understanding the UK Economy*, Macmillan.

Dale, B.G. (1992) *Total Quality and Human Resources: An Executive Guide*, Blackwell.

De Witt, B. and Meyer, R. (1994) *Strategy: Process, Content, Context*, West.

Drury, C., Braunds, S., Osborne, P. and Tayles, M. (1993) *A Survey of Management Accounting Practices in UK Manufacturing Companies*, ACCA.

Fitzgerald, L., Johnson, R., Brignall, S., Silvestio, R. and Voss, C. (1993) *Performance Measurement in Service Businesses*, CIMA.

Glad, E. and Becker, H. (1996) *Activity-based Costing and Management*, John Wiley.

Hopkins, L. (1996) 'Adventures in retail', *Accountancy Age*, 29 August.

Irvine, J. (1993) 'Justifying the imperative of change', *Accountancy*, September.

Hamel, G. and Prahalad, G. (1990) 'The core competence of the corporation', *Harvard Business Review*, May/June.

Institute of Management (1996) *Management Checklist 035: Managing Projects*, Institute of Management.

Institute of Chartered Accountants in England and Wales (1996) *Added Value Professionals: Chartered Accountants in 2005*, ICAEW.

Johnson, G. and Scholes, K. (1993) *Exploring Corporate Strategy*, Prentice Hall.

Kaplan, R.S. (1995) 'New roles for management accountants', *Journal of Cost Management*, Fall.

Kaplan, R.S. and Norton, D.P. (1992) 'The balanced scorecard: measures that drive performance', *Harvard Business Review*, January/February.

Kaplan, R.S. and Norton, D.P. (1996) 'Using the balanced scorecard as a strategic management system', *Harvard Business Review*, January/February.

Kotter, J.P. and Schlesinger, L.A. (1979) 'Choosing strategies for change', *Harvard Business Review*, March/April.

Lewin, K. (1974) 'Frontiers in group dynamics: concepts, methods and reality in social science', *Human Relations*, Vol 1.

Lord, B.R. (1996) 'Strategic management accounting: the emperor's new clothes?', *Management Accounting Research*, Vol 7.

McNamee, P.B. (1985) *Tools and Techniques for Strategic Management*, Pergamon Press.

Mintzberg, H. (1993) 'The pitfalls of strategic planning', *California Management Review*, Fall.

Obolensky, N. (1994) *Practical Business Re-engineering*, Kogan Page.

Ohmae, K. (1982) *The Mind of the Strategist*, McGraw-Hill.

Partridge, M.J. and Perren, L.J. (1994) 'Assessing and enhancing strategic capability: a value driven approach, *Management Accounting*, (UK), Vol. 72, No. 6.

Pearce, J.A. and Robinson, R.B. (1994) *Strategic Management: Formulation, Implementation and Control*, Irwin.

Pearson, G. (1990) *Strategic Thinking*, Prentice Hall.

Porter, M.E. (1979) 'How competitive forces shape strategy', *Harvard Business Review*, March/April.

Porter, M.E. (1980) *Competitive Strategy: Techniques for Analyzing Industries and Competitors*, Free Press.

Porter, M. (1985) *Competitive Advantage: Creating and Sustaining Superior Performance*, Free Press.

Rappaport, A. (1986) *Creating Shareholder Value: The New Standard for Business Performance*, Free Press.

Shank, J.K. and Govindarajan, V. (1993) *Strategic Cost Management*, Free Press.

Simmonds, K. (1981) 'Strategic management accounting', *Management Accounting* (UK), April.

Solomons, D. (1965) *Divisional Performance Measurement and Control*, Irwin.

Stacey, R.D. (1993) *Strategic Management and Organisational Dynamics*, Pitman.

Tanaka, M., Yoshikawa, T., Innes, J. and Mitchell, F. (1995) *Contemporary Cost Management*, Chapman & Hall.

Thompson, A.A. and Strickland, A.J. (1995) *Strategic Management: Concepts and Cases*, Irwin.

Townsend, R. (1985) *Further up the Organisation*, Coronet Books, Hodder & Stoughton.

Tulley, S. (1993) 'The real key to creating wealth', *Fortune*, 20 September.

Weihrich, H. (1982) 'The TOWS matrix: a tool for situational analysis', *Long Range Planning*, Vol. 15, No. 2.

Wheelen, T.L. and Hunger, J.D. (1995) *Strategic Management and Business Policy*, Addison Wesley.

Wilson, R.M.S. (1995) 'Strategic management accounting', in D. Ashton *et al.* (eds), *Issues in Management Accounting*, Prentice Hall.

Appendix D Data sources for external and industry analysis

The Macro-environment

- *Annual Abstract of Statistics*, HMSO
  400 tables of government statistics (see also the monthly digest).

- *Bank of England Quarterly Bulletin*, Bank of England
  Detailed statistics on UK monetary sector institutes.

- *Bank Reviews*, major clearing banks
  Commentary on economy and other financial issues.

- *British Humanities Index*, The Library Association
  Index of articles from over 300 periodicals.

- *Business Briefing*, British Chambers of Commerce
  Brief reports on, for example, employment, taxation, legislation, economic trends.

- *Business Strategy Review*, Oxford University Press
  Articles on current strategic issues.

- *Economic Trends*, HMSO
  UK economic data.

- *Employment Gazette*, Department of Employment
  Data on UK labour market.

- *Financial Statistics*, HMSO
  Financial data on sectors and units within the UK economy.

- *Guide to Official Statistics*, HMSO
  A comprehensive guide to government statistics.

- *Living in Britain: The General Household Survey*, HMSO
  Data on social, economic, education and health issues.

- *National Income and Expenditure*, HMSO
  Known as the Blue Book, contains comprehensive data on national income, output and expenditure.

- *Regional Trends*, HMSO
  Economic, social and demographic data by region.

- *Research Index*, Business Surveys Limited
  Index of articles in over 100 periodicals and newspapers.

- *Social Trends*, HMSO
  Details on household incomes, expenditure, demographics etc.

- *United Kingdom in Figures*, Central Statistical Office
  Data on population, employment etc.

The European Environment

- *Economic Survey of Europe*, HMSO
  Data, by country, on industry, agriculture, consumer spending, foreign trade, etc.

- *European Economy*, HMSO
  Annual review of the European Community.

The World Environment

- *OECD Economic Surveys*, HMSO
  Individual country reports.

- *World Economic Outlook*, HMSO (IMF)
  Projections and discussions for wide range of countries.

The Industry Environment

- *Business Monitor*, Business Statistics Office
  Summarised data from the annual census of statistics.

- *Business Ratios Reports*, 23 City Road, EC1Y 1AA
  Accounting data for 12,000 UK companies.

- *Dunn and Bradstreet*
  Credit status reports on quoted and unquoted UK companies.

- *Euromonitor*, Euromonitor plc
  Monthly market research reports on consumer products and services.

- *Extel*
  Provides a variety of data sources on quoted and unquoted UK companies.

- *International Marketing Data and Statistics*, Euromonitor plc
  Annual report on demographic, economic and market data.

- *Kelly's Directories*
  Provide a variety of data sources about UK firms.

- *Kompass*
  Directory of products, services and companies in the UK.

- *Marketing in Europe,* The Economist Intelligence Unit
  Market research studies of consumer goods and products.

- *Mintel Marketing Intelligence,* Mintel International Group Limited
  Monthly, bi-monthly and quarterly reports on consumer products and services.

- *Monetary Digest of Statistics,* HMSO
  Statistics on industry output.

- *Registrar of Companies*
  Keeps records of all limited companies.

- *The Centre for Interfirm Comparison*
  Comparative information about subscribing companies.

- *The Times 1000,* Times Books
  Information on the top 1,000 UK companies plus other OECD firms.

- *Who Owns Whom*
  Identifies parent companies, subsidiaries and associates.

(Extended from Griffiths, A. and Wall, S. (eds) (1995) *Applied Economics: An Introductory Course,* Longman, London.)